John Simons was born in May 1938 in Carshalton. Shortly after his birth the Simons family moved back home to St. Johns Wood, London. The reader can relive much of John's childhood through Tommy's experiences and antics.

Educated at Barrow Hill Road Primary School and Quinton Polytechnic, John did his National Service in the Army (KRRC). He spent most of his working life in London advertising agencies.

Football is his passion: he played for Merton F.C. for twenty-two years, and has been an Arsenal supporter since the age of eleven.

John and his wife Gwen are now retired and living in the lovely Welsh countryside.

BOYS FROM THE WOOD

Even though it had its share of celebrities, in the 1940's there were quite a few council flats, building sites, and bombed houses punctuating the streets of expensive houses in St. John's Wood. This was schoolboy Tommy Harris's playground. Rationing and low wages made life hard, but his working class parents were proud, and endeavoured to bring up their family to know right from wrong. With no pocket money as such, Tommy lived on his wits, finding various ways to occupy his time with his friend Tiny.

JOHN SIMONS
Co-writer:
JOAN STANLEY

◆

BOYS FROM
THE WOOD

Complete and Unabridged

ULVERSCROFT
Leicester

First published in Great Britain in 2005 by
Red'n'Ritten Ltd.
Steyning

First Large Print Edition
published 2006
by arrangement with
Red'n'Ritten Ltd.
Steyning

British Library CIP Data

Simons, John, *1938* –
    Boys from the Wood.—Large print ed.—
    Ulverscroft large print series: non-fiction
    1. Simons, John, *1938* – —Childhood and youth
    2. Large type books 3. London (England)—Social
    life and customs—20th century
    I. Title
    942.1′0854′092

    ISBN 1–84617–557–7

Published by
F. A. Thorpe (Publishing)
Anstey, Leicestershire

Set by Words & Graphics Ltd.
Anstey, Leicestershire
Printed and bound in Great Britain by
T. J. International Ltd., Padstow, Cornwall

This book is printed on acid-free paper

This book is dedicated to my late parents
Rosetta and Arthur Simons,
my brothers, sisters
and my daughter Caryn.

Illustrations

Contents

1

Saturday At Last

Wailing air raid sirens rent the air over wartime London, screaming like wounded animals over the deserted city streets. In St. John's Wood, little Tommy Harris woke with a start. He peered into the pitch darkness of the blacked-out bedroom for his older brother. Ten years his senior, Freddie was more than just a sibling to the young lad: always there at night in the tiny, shared bedroom, the sixteen-year-old provided him with a sense of security. Wartime was all Tommy could remember.

Still half asleep, desperately Tommy struggled with his trousers.

'Hurry up! And don't forget your gas mask!' Freddie's shouts served only to make him panic more. 'Everyone else has already gone down to the shelter. Why are you always the last one to wake up?'

Tommy couldn't move. He tried to run and fell over. Tears streamed down his frightened face. 'My legs! My legs! I can't walk.' In the darkness, he felt Freddie's

1

strong arms gather him up.

'Stop messing about. I'll carry you.' And with the youngster under one arm, Freddie ran out of the ground floor tenement flat, pulling the front door shut behind him.

Water poured from the broken down-pipe, and icy wetness penetrated their thin clothing. Panic stricken, Tommy struggled to move his legs, and free himself from the iron grip of his rescuer. He was getting a rough, wet ride as Freddie splashed through the puddles.

'Keep still. Or I'll end up dropping you.'

Blinding light momentarily illuminated the blacked-out streets; in the distance thunderous thuds unnerved all who heard. But this was no work of nature. This was more personal; its aim was to kill. Freddie was scared; it was too far to the air-raid shelter. After a quick glance around, he dived into the remains of a bombed out building.

He put the crying child down on the ground, peering closely at his young brother in the half-light, 'Let's have a look at you. You were OK when you went to bed last night.' Glad of an excuse to hide his own tears, he burst into laughter and rubbed his eyes, 'You idiot! No wonder you can't walk. You've put both feet down one trouser leg.'

Relief, tinged with embarrassment, surged

through Tommy's skinny body as he ruefully whispered, 'I'm sorry.'

Wet-through and cold, two brothers shared a rare and precious moment.

'Tommy, Tommy, wake up!' his mother was shaking him vigorously.

The war ended two years ago, but nine-year-old Tommy's sleep was still disturbed by memories of those war-scarred years.

'It's OK, Mum. D'yer remember when I got two legs in one trouser 'ole? That gave 'em a laugh down the shelter.'

His mother's tired eyes looked sympathetic and a wry smile hovered around her lips. 'It sounded more like a nightmare to me! Now come on, 'cos I've still got work to do. I've been up hours. Had to get yer father off to work early this morning and I've still got to sort yer sister out!'

Rose Harris was a large jovial housewife, but the stress of bringing up her family during the war, with post war rationing and tight budgeting, was beginning to show on her forty-year-old features; and a tinge of grey now ran through her hair.

Times were still hard, but she had too many bad memories not to count her blessings now the country was at peace.

'Come on, get out of that bed,' she pulled

the blankets off her young son. Saturday, the best day of the week, he felt a lot happier. No school and Saturday Morning Pictures to look forward to, all his friends would be there. Tommy jumped out of bed. He had the room to himself, and was pleased to have his own space while Freddie was away doing National Service, but he missed his brother.

'There's sixpence on there for the pictures.' His mother pointed to the sideboard.

The lad looked up from his hot porridge and pleaded, 'Can I go to the funfair at Hampstead Heath this afternoon?'

Rose's face creased in a smile, 'Of course you can, but I can't give you any more money.'

Tommy paused for a moment. 'Perhaps Dad can.'

'You'll be lucky! He keeps any spare money to himself. Anyway, he won't be home from work until late this afternoon.'

Tommy swallowed his last spoonful of breakfast, picked up his sixpence and ran out the front door.

'Make sure you're home for dinner at one o'clock.'

★ ★ ★

In another part of St. John's Wood, Arthur Harris was delivering letters. He was tired of

4

walking; the corns on his feet hurt and varicose veins made his legs ache, but it was better than being out of work. And he certainly did not want to dig up roads, as he had often done before the war.

Perspiration ran down his craggy features, he felt hot and uncomfortable in his thick uniform. Having volunteered to do overtime he would be late tonight; all he wanted was to get home and put his feet up. But it was worth it. It was good to have some loose change in his pocket for a pint of beer and a bet; bringing up four children during the war had been a struggle.

His elder daughter, Pamela, was married and his elder son was away in the Army. His thoughts turned to his two young children still at home, and he wished he could spend more time with them. 'Ah, well. Tomorrow's Sunday and we can all be together for a change.'

★ ★ ★

Walking up Finchley Road to the Odeon at Swiss Cottage, Tommy was deep in thought. 'How can I get some money for the funfair?'

Tommy was a bit of a celebrity with the rest of the lads; a few weeks previously, he had won a Just William competition on the stage at the Odeon. He would never forget it. His prize, an inscribed scouts knife, was presented to him with an embarrassing kiss on the cheek by fifteen-year-old child-star Petula Clark. He was even photographed and interviewed by the local paper, The Marylebone Mercury. They described him as 'The ultimate, scruffy schoolboy portrayed in the Richmal Crompton books.' He felt quite proud, and for a few days he enjoyed a modicum of fame, as people he did not even know recognised him in the street and stopped to talk to him.

Tiny was standing outside the cinema with some other kids. Thin and gangly, with slightly protruding teeth, he was about six inches taller than anyone else. 'All right, Tommy?'

'Yeah . . . ' Tommy's voice trailed off. He had a brilliant idea. 'I'll get all the tickets, it'll save you all queuing up.'

He quickly collected sixteen tanners, but when he reached the ticket office Tommy asked the cashier for, 'Twelve please, Miss.'

He rejoined his friends, and carefully folded the strip of tickets into the size of one. 'Follow me.' Approaching the usherette on the door he offered them to her, 'Sixteen please, Miss.'

The usherette smiled, 'You're the little lad

who was Just William, aren't you?'

Tommy nodded as she tore the tickets in half and beckoned him and his friends through the door. He had a grin as big as a Cheshire cat, 'Now I can go to the funfair.'

The organ rose from its pit, with the organist, a jolly, ginger haired man, playing 'We come along on Saturday morning greeting everyone with a smile.' With the ping-pong balls bouncing along the words on the screen Tommy and his friends joined in the customary sing-a-long before immersing themselves in a programme of cartoons and films that fed their childhood fantasies. A cowboy film always came last; Tommy realised long ago that the 'baddies' wore black hats, whereas the 'goodies' were white.

Engrossed in the film, Tommy did not notice the usherette shining a torch along the different rows of seats until the light blinded him.

'Come on, you two! Just William and your mate! Out!'

Tommy's heart sank as he and Tiny got up.

'What's this all about?'

Tommy shrugged.

Tiny was indignant, 'We'll miss the end of the film.'

'Just William and your mate! Out!'

Waving her torch as a guiding light, the usherette led them back to the foyer. 'How many tickets are there?' She held out her hand to reveal the torn halves of Tommy's tickets.

Tiny was genuinely puzzled.

Very guiltily, Tommy looked at the floor. 'Twelve, Miss.'

The usherette nodded. 'And how many did you say there was?'

'Sixteen, Miss.'

'So you owe me two shillings, don't you?'

Tommy reluctantly put his hand in his pocket and handed over the four tanners.

'Now what shall I do with you? A few weeks ago you were the centre of attention as Just William, but even he wouldn't do what you've just done. You wouldn't like to see this in the local newspaper, would you? Shall I call the police or tell your parents?'

Frightened and tearful Tommy begged, 'Please don't tell anyone. I won't do it again. I just wanted some money for the fair.'

'All right. But I'm not letting you back in. You can miss the end of the film. Next time it will be the police station for you.'

'Thank you, Miss. I won't do it again, Miss. Honest, Miss.'

Tommy was relieved, until he got outside and Tiny got hold of him.

'You idiot!'

'I was only trying . . . '

'You'll get us locked up one day.'

After ten minutes of heated argument the lights came up and the kids started coming out of the cinema.

'What happened?'

'Why did she drag you both out?'

'You missed the end of the film. The goodies won.'

'Don't they always? We didn't bother to go back in, we knew what'd happen.' Tommy tried to sound relaxed. 'I'm Roy Rogers!'

A few seconds later they were all playing their favourite games as heroes of the Wild West. And Tommy wasn't Tommy anymore. Running in and out of the derelict, bombed houses in Finchley Road, hiding in doorways, shooting each other with their fingers, each took on another persona.

Cries of 'Bang! Bang! You're dead!'

And, 'You missed!' rang out in the Saturday morning air.

★   ★   ★

Their friends having gone their separate ways, the two pals walked along the street. 'Going to the funfair this afternoon, Tiny?

Unhappily Tiny kicked a stone into the

10

gutter. 'Yeah, but I haven't got any money.'

Tommy grinned, 'Nor have I, but I've just thought of a way of getting some.' He pointed to the off-licence across the road. 'Look, some of the yard fence is missing. We can climb through and get some soda siphons, and take them back for the two bob deposit.'

Running in and out of the traffic, ignoring the shouts of several angry motorists, they raced across the road. Two boys ran out of the off-licence, chased by an angry, red faced, shopkeeper. Outpaced, the tubby man stopped and pointed to the boys as they disappeared into a distant alley. 'Blooming rogues! They tried giving me back my own soda-siphons. They must think I was born yesterday.'

His face reddened to a beetroot hue; he waved his arms about and spluttered, 'And look what they have done to my fence!'.

Tommy thought the licensee was about to burst a blood vessel. In mock innocence he empathised, 'That's terrible. Can we help in any way?'

'If you two can help me mend that fence I'll give you a couple of bob each.'

The boys' faces lit up. Their financial problems solved for another day. 'Of course, what can we do, Mister?'

'Mr. Perkins to you.'

The man disappeared inside the shop and returned with a hammer and some nails. 'I just need you to hold the panels while I nail them back in place.'

Half an hour later, in the bright warm sunshine, the fence looked almost new. Gratefully, Mr. Perkins thanked the boys and pressed a florin into each outstretched, sweaty hand.

'That was lucky, weren't it? Come on let's go home. I'll meet you at two o'clock and we'll go to the funfair.'

★ ★ ★

'Where have you been?' His six-year-old sister was standing at the back door chewing the end of one of her pigtails.

'You know I go to Saturday morning flicks.'

Shirley sulked. 'Why don't you take me?'

Tommy sighed, 'I've told you before, you're not old enough until next year. And anyway, you were still fast asleep in bed when I went out.'

Shirley stuck out her tongue and ran inside. 'Mummy, Tommy's home.' Tommy took off his coat and followed her into the kitchen.

Rose was dishing up their dinner. 'About time, too. You're late!'

'Sorry, Mum, but we helped Mr. Perkins at the off-licence mend his fence, and he gave us two bob each as a reward.'

Rose looked suspicious. 'You telling the truth?'

With a mouthful of dumpling Tommy protested, 'Honest, Mum. You can check up if you like!'

'Hmm!' His mother was not convinced, but she shrugged her shoulders and let it pass. 'Shirley's been nagging me to let her go to the fair, but I told her she's too young. Maybe next year.'

★ ★ ★

Tommy breathed a sigh of relief, and rushed out of the house. Tiny was waiting, as arranged, outside the newsagents, at the top of the street. They walked towards Hampstead Heath, the sun still warm on their faces. 'I thought for one dreadful minute that I was going to get lumbered with my little sister.'

'That's the last thing we want: a soppy little girl hanging around with us!'

Tommy nodded in agreement. 'Yeah. My big brother reckons I'll change my mind about girls when I'm older. But I don't think so.'

'I know. Ain't it funny how big boys are

always chasing after girls. All that kissing and cuddling and stuff.'

Tommy pulled a face. 'I think it's something you only do before you get married, 'cos I never see my Mum and Dad doing it.' He paused thoughtfully. 'Anyway, they take their teeth out after dinner. I hate going to the bathroom and seeing their teeth soaking in a glass.'

Tiny nodded thoughtfully, 'That's it! It's probably 'orrible kissing with no teeth.'

★   ★   ★

They could hear all the sounds of the fair a mile away: the hurdy-gurdy music accompanying the children's screams, as they enjoyed the bitter-sweet thrill of the scary rides, and the raucous cries of the travelling barkers. Excited, Tommy and Tiny rushed towards the enticing noise.

They were soon caught up in the fun of the fair: sliding down the helter-skelter, bumping into each other on the dodgems, and riding the carousels. 'We've got four bob.'

'Yeah. That's . . . ' Tiny thought hard, but arithmetic was not his strong point. 'How much are they charging for a ride?'

'Tuppence.' Tommy picked up a stone and scratched some sums on the ground. 'Twelve pence to the shilling. We've got four, so that's forty-eight. Divided by two . . . Cor! That's twelve rides *each!*'

Totally unconcerned with logic, Tiny was more interested in its potential. 'I know! Let's go on the ghost train.'

They rattled through tunnel after tunnel. Weird sound effects and skeletons jumped out of the darkness, but they were not frightened at all. 'Not very good, is it?' Tiny shouted over the noise of the machinery and other people's screams.

Tommy grinned wickedly. 'Let's get out and hide behind a skeleton.'

No sooner had they tucked themselves behind a gruesome model when a car full of young girls came through. The two boys jumped out screaming and wailing, and ran back to the entrance past the startled attendants as a group of frightened, crying girls came out the other end.

Once clear of the ghost train Tommy and Tiny stopped running. 'That was great, wasn't it?' Tiny breathlessly agreed.

'We haven't got much money left. Let's buy some ice-creams.'

Tiny bit off the pointed end of his cornet and sucked hard, his cheeks quite hollow until they filled with the deliciously cold mixture.

'What yer doing that for?' Tommy asked.

'I don't like being left with the dry biscuit stuff when the ice-cream's gone.'

Tommy tried it. 'Good, ain't it?'

'Yeah. Watch out. You're losing it down yourself. You have to keep you mouth over the hole or it will run out.'

But Tommy wasn't interested. A deep gruff voice rang out, 'Every one's a winner!'

He pointed to the rifle range. 'Every one's a winner, Tiny. Come on let's have a go.'

'Last one there's a sissy!' They raced through the crowd to the stall and picked out a couple of rifles. The man in charge held out his hand for their thruppenny bits still shouting, 'Any bull's-eye wins a prize.'

Tiny shot hopelessly wide of the mark. Tommy covetously eyed the toys on display. Placing the rifle to his shoulder, very carefully he took aim. He missed. And he missed the second shot. But with his third shot he hit a bulls-eye. Jumping up in the air excitedly he shouted out to the stallholder, 'I'll have that toy aeroplane.'

The man laughed. 'You only get those prizes if you get three bulls-eyes.' He went behind a curtain and brought out a small cardboard box with two little mice in it. 'Here y'are.'

Tommy was disappointed and annoyed. 'Let's go home.'

Tiny put his finger through the cage, and tried to stroke them. 'They're great. What are you going to call 'em?'

'Doom and Gloom. If my Dad sees 'em, they're dead. He caught one in our back yard and flushed it down the lav'.'

Despondently they trudged back over Hampstead Heath kicking fallen twigs and leaves, and headed for St. John's Wood and home.

* * *

At the bottom of Ordnance Hill, Tommy said goodbye to his friend. 'See you tomorrow.'

How could he hide two white mice? He went back to his parents' ground floor council flat. A colourful assortment of laundry items and various sheets hung from the washing line, festooning the back yard. He put the cardboard cage containing the mice on his bedroom window ledge, went round to the front door and knocked, shouting through the letterbox, 'It's only me, Mum!'

Rose opened the door. 'What have you been up to?'

'Nothing!' Tommy replied guiltily, fooling his mother wasn't easy. He hurried to his bedroom.

17

'Make sure you wash yourself before tea! Yer father'll be home soon.'

Tommy opened his bedroom window and retrieved the box. Opening it, he saw a small hole where the mice had been chewing the cardboard. 'You're not safe in here.' He stroked one, enjoying the warmth and softness of its pure white fur. 'What are we going to do with you? What you need is a house of your own.'

Then an idea struck him. His face lit up. Hearing his sister and mother talking in the kitchen he crept along the hallway to Shirley's bedroom. After a few minutes he came out and went to the bathroom and pulled the chain — to give himself an alibi. 'What's for tea?'

'Condensed milk sandwiches.'

Tommy sniffed the air. 'I'm starving, what's that I can smell cooking?'

'Don't be greedy. You've had your dinner, that's yer father's. He'll be famished when he gets home.'

Tommy sat down, next to his little sister. She stuck her tongue out through the thick, sticky, condensed milk dripping from her lips. 'Greedy pig!'

He ignored her and hungrily tucked into his tea.

Wearily his father entered the kitchen. Rose

looked lovingly at him. 'Had a hard day, luv?'

Resignedly, Arthur took off his glasses and wiped his eyes. 'Not 'arf! Never stopped all day.'

She put a plate of rabbit stew and dumplings in front of him. 'Get stuck into that lot, while I get Shirley to bed. She's falling asleep over her tea.'

'No! No! I don't want to go to bed.'

But her mother remained firm. 'Go and wash your face and hands. And put your pyjamas on. I'll be with you in a minute.' Sulkily, Shirley left the kitchen.

Moments later her screams echoed through the flat. Tommy's face fell. His father nearly choked on a piece of rabbit, and his mother ran down the hall to Shirley's bedroom.

The screams ceased. There was an eerie silence before Rose stormed back into the kitchen, making a beeline for her son. 'It's you, Tommy Harris, ain't it? There's bleedin' mice in her dolls house.' She clipped him around the ear.

Defiantly Tommy cried out, 'I won them at the fair, don't let Dad kill them.' He streaked down the hall followed by his parents.

Shirley was standing on her bed crying her eyes out. 'Mummy, Mummy, they've got out.' Pointing to the floor, 'They ran under the bed.' Everyone got down on all fours frantically searching for the escapees.

Arthur saw them run out of the bedroom. 'There they go.' With a broom in his hands, he tried to hit the terrified creatures.

Tommy ran into the hall, opened the front door and let the mice run out. 'You can't get them now.'

His father's face reddened with anger. 'That's it. It's an early night for you, my lad. And you're not going out tomorrow!' He returned to his daughter's room where Rose was comforting the young child.

Tommy was philosophical about it all. He shrugged his shoulders. 'What a day! Just wait till I get to school on Monday. I bet no-one had a Saturday like mine.'

2

An Apple A Day

Deep below ground, not a sound disturbed the night. A sleepless body tossed and turned on its hard bunk, one of many lining the basement walls. The air, a mixture of damp mustiness, human body odours and, occasionally, a pleasant waft of sweet perfume, was penetrated by a strong, descending, cold draught.

A shout cut through the eerie silence disturbing the strained peace. More shouting. People raised themselves, running through the building and up the slope to street level, and the basement in Oslo Court disgorged its occupants. Leaving the shelter, Tommy and his brother followed and joined the throng gazing up into the sky.

Tommy picked out a trail of stars shooting through the darkness. No, not stars! He rubbed his sleepy eyes, the better to focus on the drama being acted out above his head.

A Spitfire was shooting at something — smaller than a normal plane. He tugged at his brother's sleeve, 'What's that?'

'Don't yer know? It's one of them

21

doodlebug things.'

'It ain't very big. Where's the driver?'

'Pilot! It don't need one. It's a flying bomb. When the engine stops, it'll suddenly drop out of the sky and explode.'

Colour drained from Tommy's face. He felt sick.

'Don't worry. The Spitfire pilot'll get it. He'll make it explode in midair . . . '

For the first time, the terrified boy heard the urgent shouts of the crowd. In his need to release his fear, and as though the pilot's efforts depended on his nervous energy, Tommy shrieked, 'Go on, get him. Get him . . . '

'Tommy, you'll be late for school.' His mother was shouting at him. 'I'm fed up with getting complaints from them teachers of yours.'

Blearily he opened his eyes. 'It's not my fault. I always have to wait for Shirley.'

'Don't blame your sister. You're as bad as each other!'

Mechanically he went through the process of getting up and having his breakfast. Rose held up a shiny pair of shoes. 'And another thing, what have you been doing to your school shoes?'

'Eh?'

'There's holes in the soles, again.'

'Nothing.'

'I've stuffed a bit of cardboard in them. It'll have to do until I can afford to take 'em to the cobbler's.'

Silently, Tommy put them on. Good old Mum; at least she had cleaned them, saving him a job. She gave her children a quick inspection.

'You'll do, off you go, both of you.'

'Have you got any sweets, Mum?'

Their mother waved the ration book at them. 'Sorry, no coupons left. We've used 'em all up for this week.'

But Shirley pouted, 'That's not fair. I haven't had any for *ages*.'

'You'll survive. Here's your dinner money, be satisfied with that. There's many a child'd be glad to . . . '

Rose Harris smiled, her homily left unfinished she watched her youngsters quickly pocket the cash and run off down the road hand in hand. It gladdened her heart to know that they were close, despite the occasionally bickering.

★   ★   ★

They pushed open the squeaky, rusty school gate and, just as the bell rang, they ran across the playground. At the old red brick building they went their separate ways.

'See you later.' Tommy waved to his sister

23

and made his way to his classroom.

Sad faced, Tiny was already there. 'Another boring old day.'

Tommy nodded and thought for a moment. 'I know! Let's go scrumping at lunchtime.'

Tiny was horrified, 'You're joking ain't yer? My Mum'll kill me! Remember what happened last time?'

Tommy looked disappointed, 'Yeah, I got a clip round the ear and wasn't allowed out for three days.' The boys gazed at each other, deep in thought.

'My Dad told me where Bernard Miles lives, he's famous, and my Dad delivers letters there.'

Tiny shrugged his shoulders. 'He's not that famous.'

'He is! I saw him in Great Expectations at the flicks and my Dad laughs at him on the wireless. I bet we can get his autograph.'

Tiny shook his head. 'I bet we can't. He won't be in or one of his servants will send you away. But at least it will be a bit of a laugh.'

'Just 'cos he's famous, don't mean he's got servants,' Tommy smirked.

A sudden silence descended on the classroom as Mr. Phipps, the English teacher entered. A big burly man with curly hair and glasses, he glared threateningly at anyone who looked as though their lips were moving.

Somehow, Tommy got through the morning's lessons without incident and unscathed. Mr. Phipps had a habit of throwing the wooden-backed board duster at any child he thought wasn't paying attention. Through hours of practice, Tommy had perfected a very thoughtful look while his mind was absorbed with something else.

At last, the lunchtime bell sounded. Everyone put their books away and rushed out of the building.

'What now?' Tiny enquired.

'Bernard Miles lives in Acacia Road. I've got these for his autograph.' Tommy produced a pencil and a page from an old exercise book.

Tiny was hungry, 'Let's get some chips first.' Smiling to himself, 'Our Mums would go potty if they knew we spent out dinner money on chips.'

Tommy sniggered and pulled a face, 'But the school dinners are 'orrible.'

'Yeah, the greens are like blotting paper.'

'And the tapioca . . . '

'Frogspawn,' they laughed. Hardly an original thought; there was not a school child around who didn't give that pudding, particularly popular with those who drew up school menus, it's graphic nickname.

Hurriedly, they unwrapped the newspaper

and dipped their fingers into red-hot chips. Both boys were of the opinion that chips didn't taste half so good off a plate. Burnt fingers and sore mouths were a small price to pay.

* * *

Heading for Acacia Road, they walked through St. John's Wood. The scars of war were everywhere to be seen. Each street had a building site or bombed out buildings that proved irresistible to the two boys. They took shortcuts, running and kicking stones across the debris, until they reached a big iron gate outside a house on the corner of Ordnance Hill and Acacia Road.

They pushed the gate open and started to walk up the very long, winding gravel path. Tommy was limping.

'What's wrong?' Tiny asked anxiously.

Tommy leant on his friend. 'Some stones have gone through the cardboard in my shoes. Hang on a minute while I shake 'em out.'

'Look' Excitedly, Tiny pointed at an apple tree with its branches hanging over a large garden shed.

Tommy followed his friend's gaze. 'Whopping great red apples! I bet they're good.'

'Yeah.'

'You OK?'

'We could climb up onto that old shed and pick a couple.'

Giving into temptation they walked over to the shed; Tommy climbed onto the roof and started to pick the mouth-watering fruit. The roof creaked ominously. Tommy hesitated for a moment, and his feet sensed the inevitable. He plunged through tarmac and wood; his descent somewhat more hasty and undignified than his ascent a few minutes earlier. A large bright red shiny apple in each hand he had no means of breaking his fall, and left gravity to do its worst.

A worried and frightened Tiny opened the shed door. Nervously he went in, looking for his friend in the semi-darkness, 'You OK?'

Covered in bits of decaying vegetation, Tommy emerged from a pile of old grass cuttings. He got up slowly; testing to make sure his legs would take his weight. They were a bit wobbly, but otherwise they seemed all right. He got up wiping a bit of blood, from a cut on his cheek, across his face, and brushed compost out of his hair and clothes. 'I think so.'

'You look like a scarecrow.' Tiny wasn't sure if he was going to laugh or cry, he was so relieved to see that his chum hadn't done himself any serious harm. 'What have you done with them apples?'

'All right, lads?' A rosy-cheeked man in

gumboots stood framed in the doorway: the gardener, no doubt.

Feeling trapped Tommy panicked. 'Sorry, Mister, we only wanted a few apples.'

The man roared with laughter, 'It's OK as long as you've no broken bones. I've been meaning to have that roof fixed for a long time.' Tommy and Tiny shielded their eyes as they came out into the bright sunlight. 'What are you doing here, anyway?'

Tommy reached into his pocket, 'We were going to ask Bernard Miles for his autograph.'

The man smiled, 'Well, that's no problem,' and taking the pencil and much folded piece of paper he leant it against the shed and signed his name twice. He then carefully tore the sheet in two and gave the pieces back.

The boys were astonished, 'You're Bernard Miles?'

'That's right, boys. You only had to come to the house; if you wanted a few apples as well you only had to ask. We can't use them all, most just fall off and rot on the ground. Take as many as you want before you go, but remember it's only right that you always ask permission first.'

Tommy's eyes lit up. 'Thanks, Mr. Miles, we are really sorry.'

The boys gathered up the fruit that had fallen through the shed roof and watched

Bernard Miles make his way back to the house.

Their shirts bulging with apples, they made their way back to the main road. At the top of the road Tommy smiled and looked back. 'That was great, wasn't it?'

Struggling to keep most of his apples inside his shirt, Tiny agreed. 'Yeah, what a nice bloke. I thought we were really in trouble.'

Tommy's smile changed to a frown. 'I bet my Mum won't believe what happened. She'll probably give me a clout round the ear for scrumping.'

Tiny pulled an apple out from his shirt and wiped it on his sleeve. Biting into its bright red skin, 'I never thought of that. We'll just have to show them the autographs as evidence.'

Happily they hurried back to school munching their loot. When they arrived back at the school there was nobody to be seen. They were later than they thought. The front of both boys' shirts were bulging, and like two Billy Bunter figures they crossed the empty playground to the school entrance. 'I know, Tiny, push the apples round to your back, so when we go into the classroom the teacher won't see them.'

A tired-looking Miss Beck, the music teacher, sternly looked over her glasses. 'You two! You're late, the headmaster wants to see you in his study.'

Tommy and Tiny looked at each other gloomily, and retreated backwards from the classroom. They walked down the corridor to the principal's office, knocked his door and entered. A bald man with a moustache, looked at them; clearly vexed he demanded, 'Why were you two back late from lunch?'

'Sorry, sir,' Tommy offered meekly, 'We were playing over the park and didn't realise the time.'

While the headmaster pondered, the boys were nervously trying to keep their apples to the back of their shirts with their arms. Mistaking their peculiar behaviour for contrition, the head master was satisfied, this time. 'Don't let it happen again or you'll be in line for the cane!'

Instead of turning and running, they backed towards the door slowly and out into the corridor. The headmaster looked puzzled then shook his head. He liked his pupils to be frightened of him, but he was not used to being treated like royalty. 'Boys!'

'Phew! That was close.'

'Yeah. Once we're in class we'll hide the apples in our desks till going home time.'

They entered the classroom and from Miss

Beck's desk they just looked like a couple of sheepish lads returning from the head's study, but from the rear they resembled little hunchbacks. Fortunately they sat at the back of the class, and only a few of their classmates noticed.

★   ★   ★

The rest of the afternoon dragged on. Mr. Barlow, the Maths teacher, a stern upright figure of a man took over from Miss Beck. Tommy quite liked sums, and seemed to satisfy the teacher with his answers.

★   ★   ★

At long last the sound of the 'going home' bell rang through the corridors. While most of the children rushed for the door Tommy and Tiny made a pretence of tidying up their desks. With the lids balanced on their heads they furtively stuffed the apples back into their shirts.

A sharp elbow in the ribs reminded the chums that there was a price to pay for silence, and a payoff was duly accepted.

Leaving the classroom the boys assessed the situation. 'What are you going to tell your Mum?'

'What about?'

'The apples, idiot!'

'Oh, I dun'no.' Tommy thought it over for a while. 'I'll tell her the truth and hope that she believes me. At least they will get eaten and not rot away in a garden.'

Tiny nodded his approval.

Outside in the playground some boys were playing conkers. Tommy had given the game up some time ago. He smiled as he remembered the champion conker he used to have, and how his little sister had told everyone that he had soaked it in vinegar and baked it in the oven.

Shirley was waiting impatiently at the school gates. 'Where have you been? And what's under your shirts?'

Tommy teased, 'Nothing.'

'Yes there is. I'll tell Mum.

Tommy looked heavenwards. 'They're apples for Mum, stupid!'

Peanut Annie stood at the gates, as usual, with her rusty Smith's Crisp tin, and her Jack Russell, selling crisps and peanuts at tuppence a bag.

'I want some crisps.'

'You'll have to wait for your tea 'cos I haven't got any money.' Tommy was frightened of Peanut Annie, anyway. She reminded him of the witch in 'The Wizard Of Oz'.

* * *

Tommy took the key from under the doormat. He knew his mother would be at her cleaning job, five days a week — sometimes mornings, sometimes afternoons — she worked for Dorothy Carless, a singer who was quite famous.

He took all his apples from his shirt and put them in a bowl on the kitchen sideboard. Despite his confident attitude with Tiny he was anticipating his mother's reaction with a fair degree of anxiety.

'Can I have an apple?'

'No!' Tommy said sternly. 'Mum'll be home soon. So wait for your tea.'

Shirley pulled a sulky face. 'I'll tell her you don't go to school dinners.'

His face fell, 'Oh, all right, but eat it quick before Mum comes home.' Still worried, Tommy took off his jacket and went into the bedroom.

Half an hour later he heard Rose coming in. His sister ran to the door to greet her. 'Mummy, Mummy, Tommy's got some apples!'

Feeling glum, he entered the kitchen, 'Let's get this over with'. Some apples had fallen off the dish. Their presence seemed to dominate the kitchen.

'What have you been up to, Tommy?' Arms akimbo, mouth pursed, her anger was thinly veiled. 'Look at the state of you! You've got scratches on your face and legs. Your shoes are filthy. You have been scrumping again, haven't you?'

Tommy cut a long story short by telling a little white lie, 'No, honest, Mum, I fell over on some gravel when me and Tiny went round to Bernard Miles's house for his autograph.'

He paused for breath and to measure his mother's mood. 'Honestly, we haven't been scrumping, Mum. He told us we could have the apples as he has too many and they only fall on the ground and rot.' With a pleading look in his eyes he held out a piece of paper. 'Look, here's where he signed. It's the truth, Mum.'

Mrs. Harris looked doubtful. 'I'll believe you, but thousands wouldn't. And if you're lying you'll have your father to deal with!'

Despite the suspicious look on her face, as most mothers are wont, Rose felt protective towards her brood and often showed a softer side where they were concerned. All kids pinched fruit out of gardens at some time, and she didn't see it as particularly bad behaviour: just a 'boys will be boys!' type of thing. And the apples certainly were lovely and rosy-red: much better than the ones in the shops.

Sternly she looked at her youngest son and wagged her finger. 'OK, but for goodness sake, Tommy, be careful what you get up to.' Then remembering that she had been wondering what she could find to make a pudding for her work-worn husband, she smiled. 'Anyway, your Dad loves apple pie.'

Tommy couldn't believe his luck. 'If I can have a bit, you're the best Mum in the world.'

She cuffed the air above his head, and turned on her heel before he saw the smile she couldn't hide.

3

Rags To Riches

'This is smashing, Mum. Your stew is the best in all the world.'

'What are you after?' Freddie reached across the dinner table to ruffle his little brother's hair.

'Nothing.'

'Or should I say, what have you . . . '

Without warning, the all too familiar screams of the air raid siren silenced the squabbling lads.

Mrs. Harris was first to react. 'Quick!'

Like a well-rehearsed drill the family grabbed their plates of food and ran down the hall to the front door. They had done this all through the war, since the day their mother had reasoned, 'If we are near the front door it will be easier for them to dig us out!'

Tommy just accepted it. Like so many times before, they closed their eyes, crossed their fingers and prayed. The constant drone of a doodlebug, somewhere in the distance, gradually increased in intensity as *it got nearer and nearer. Without warning the engine stopped . . . They held their breath: the deadly silence went on forever . . . before a loud explosion, some distance away, rattled the doors and windows. The family opened their eyes and thanked God that they were still alive. But somewhere someone's war had ended, along with their lives.*

Tommy screamed with relief . . .

He woke in a sweat. His mother stood over his bed with a worried look on her face, 'I heard you scream, another nightmare?'

Tommy managed a brave smile, 'Don't worry, mum. I'm getting used to them now.' Secretly, he wondered when he would stop having these flashbacks of war.

She beckoned him to the window, 'Come on, get up it's snowing outside.' Tommy jumped out of bed, it was half term, November 1947, and he had a few days off school.

He washed and dressed and sat down to breakfast with his sister. 'Here you are, some nice hot porridge.'

'Why can't I have some eggs and bacon like Dad?' Tommy sulked.

'Because we hardly get any at all with the rationing, anyway porridge is much better for you this freezing cold weather.' Knowing this argument would cut no ice with her younger son she tried, 'Your father works blooming hard for this family, and if I didn't go out to work we'd wouldn't have what we do get. Just you be satisfied.' Then she shook her head sadly, 'You'll understand when you get older.'

Tommy looked downcast and muttered under his breath, 'When I grow up I'm going to have lots of bacon and eggs.'

'I'm taking yer sister round to Auntie Maud's before I go to work, I'll be back for dinner, but I want you to take that old pram in the passage down to Lisson Grove and get as much nutty slack as you can this morning.'

Tommy pulled a face; he hated being sent to the railway marshalling yard to collect fuel, it was a filthy job. The black, gritty dust got everywhere: in your hair and your eyes and, if you were not careful, in your mouth as well.

His mother pointed at him, 'Look! Don't be a lazy little sod, we all pull our weight in this house, so don't argue.' Looking out the window she continued, 'If this weather carries on we're going to need all the coal we can get!'

After breakfast Tommy put on the biggest jumper he could find, which wasn't hard as most of his clothes were hand-me-downs from Freddie, and a thick scarf and large overcoat. As arranged he met Tiny at ten o'clock.

Hands in his pockets, his friend was stamping cold feet on the snow-covered pavement. 'What do you need that for?'

Tommy's face reflected his misery, 'I've got to go down the rail yard — you know — where they keep the coal for the trains, and see how much nutty slack I can get for my Mum.'

Tiny moaned disappointedly, 'That's not much fun, I thought we were going up Primrose Hill to have a snowball fight.'

The boys' disappointment hung in the air like their frozen breath.

'Sorry I've got to go.' But then his face lit up, 'Look, we could go and collect old clothes at the posh flats and take them to the rag and bone man in Church Street.'

'Yeah, we could make some money and buy some sweets.'

'But we haven't any coupons.'

'No problem! I know a shop that sells them without coupons if you pay more money.'

Gleefully, they set off around St Johns Wood. An hour or so later they had filled the pram. Tommy held up a ragged old frock. 'You wouldn't think posh people would have clothes in this state, would you?'

Stopping at the greengrocers they managed to cadge an old potato sack. 'Lets put some old bits of brick in some of the clothes. He hardly ever opens the sacks, he just weighs 'em and pays so much a pound. If they weigh more, we'll get more money!' Tiny laughed and nodded in agreement.

Wheeling the well loaded pram through the snow and ice to Church Street was hard work, and a bit smelly.

★   ★   ★

Like a post war Fagin, a round shouldered, unshaven old man with matted hair, scruffy clothes and mittens, ushered them into his emporium. 'Come in lads, what have you got there?'

The shop was littered with old rags, newspapers and some objects that were unrecognisable, and it had a musty smell. He lifted the sack from the pram and put it on his huge scales, weighing it carefully. 'Hmmm, that's about twelve pounds! That's a bit heavier than I thought.'

To the boys' dismay he peered inside the sack and then felt into various pockets. Holding a piece of brick before their eyes he

41

'What's this?'

demanded, 'What's this?'

'We didn't know they were there, honest mister.'

As the old man emptied the sack of clothes and upturned it the remaining stones fell to the ground. Through a cloud of dust his eyes narrowed and looked at Tommy disbelievingly, 'Sure!'

He pondered for a few moments, 'As you tried to trick me, I'll only give you half the normal rate to teach you a lesson.' He quickly gathered up the clothes, weighed them and pushed half a crown into Tommy's hand, 'Now clear off and think yourselves lucky I didn't call the police.'

At the bridge overlooking the rail yard Tiny gave an ironic smile, 'We were lucky back there, and now all we've got to do is carry this pram down those steps to the railway lines without anyone seeing us. Or are you determined to get us nicked?'

'Don't worry, I've done it before. If the rail men see you they still let you have the nutty slack 'cos it ain't much use to them. Anyway my Mum says they turn a blind eye 'cos they're working class and their kids have probably got their arse hanging out of their trousers just like us.'

Picking up the pieces of nutty slack through the snow made their woollen gloves soaking wet. Their hands were freezing. Carrying the empty pram down the steps was easy enough, but once the pram was loaded they had the treacherous and heavy job of carrying it back up the ice encrusted steps, one by one, to street level. With great relief they eventually reached Lisson Grove.

'I can't feel my fingers.' Tommy threw his soaking wet gloves into the pram and seeking warmth thrust his hands deep into his overcoat pockets.

Tiny followed suit: welcoming the tingling feeling and the pain that follows the numbness of intense cold. Neither boy was willing to put bare hands on the freezing pram handles.

'It'll be easier now. We'll take it in turns.'

So sharing their discomfort in the biting cold wind the boys wheeled the nutty slack to the other end of St Johns Wood.

As they passed Lords Cricket Ground they remembered better climes, 'We had some good times bunking in there in the summer, didn't we, Tiny?'

His pal smiled, 'Compton and Edrich were great, can't wait until next summer. It seems a long way away with this weather don't it?'

At last they reached the Harris's flat. 'I'll take this round to the backyard and put it in the coal shed. If I come out later I'll call for you. All right?'

Tommy took the key from under the mat and went indoors. 'I've put the nutty slack and pram in the shed, Mum.'

'Oi! Put the wood in the hole! It's bloody freezing!'

Turning to shut the front door, 'Is that all the thanks I get? I hate that job. I'm freezing.'

'And look at the state of you, get those wet things off and jump in a hot bath.'

While he waited for the bath to fill, Tommy looked at his shivering coal black reflection in the mirror and realised just how cold and wet he was.

★ ★ ★

Glowing from his hot bath, Tommy gratefully wolfed the beef stew and bread his mother set before him. 'Mum, can I go out this afternoon?'

'I don't think that's a good idea, Son. It's gone two o'clock now and it'll be dark soon.'

Tommy pulled a face, 'I said I'd call for Tiny.'

'No! Look at the weather, there's a blizzard out there.' Dreamily she looked out of the window, 'I hope it's not like this when Princess Elizabeth gets married next week.

45

People dream of a white Christmas, but it's not what they want when they talk of a white wedding.'

Tommy's ears pricked up, 'I could write a letter to Father Christmas this afternoon, couldn't I?' His excitement rising as he thought of the forthcoming celebrations, 'If I put it up the chimney early I might get everything I ask for.'

Last year, he remembered, he only got the toy soldiers he had asked for and not the big fort that went with them.

His mother gently put her hand on his shoulder, 'Don't expect too much, even Father Christmas has to ration out his presents, you know.' One day he would find out the truth just as she had as a child.

Fortunately in St John's Wood there was a real-life post war Father Christmas called Doctor Geortze, a German Jew, who lived in a big house on the edge of Regents Park. He supplied all the local poor families with a Christmas Hamper, for which Tommy's mother, along with a lot of others were very grateful.

'I'm going to collect Shirley from Auntie Maud's before it gets too dark.' His mother put on her coat and opened the front door. 'Ugh, this weather! Your father will be frozen to the marrow by the time he gets home,' she muttered as she closed the door behind her.

Tommy shrugged his shoulders and disappeared into his bedroom, counting the days to Christmas he was eager to write his note to Father Christmas before his little sister got home.

4

Christmas Presents

'Silent night, Holy Night . . . ' Defiantly the Christmas carol echoed around the air raid shelter in Oslo Court; everyone joined in.

Shooting stars lit up the night sky and explosions echoed in the distance. But this was not November and the display was not put on for entertainment. Overhead the Royal Air Force and the Luftwaffe were locked in mortal combat.

Mrs. Harris shook her head sadly. 'I wish it was a bloody silent night! What a way to spend Christmas Eve.'

In damp and cold Tommy and Shirley huddled together, shivering, on a single bunk beneath a solitary blanket. His older brother and sister joined in with the carollers.

'What's so special about Christmas, it's just like any other time of the . . . '

Tommy's thoughts were drowned out by a crying woman's tearful screams as she ran into the shelter . . .

His mother noticed Tommy's silent mood, 'You had another one of them blooming nightmares?'

He nodded, 'Do you remember that Christmas when Mrs. Johnson came running back down the shelter after her house had been bombed.'

'I'll never forget it, she lost her parents that day. It was the only time they never came down the shelter. The bombing sounded so bad she went back to persuade them to come down, but it was too late.'

'Where was Father Christmas in the war, Mum?'

'It was too dangerous for him to go round the World, he stayed at home in Greenland during the war. And don't forget there was rationing. Not even Father Christmas could control Hitler, son.'

★   ★   ★

Lessons that morning were used to make decorations to brighten up the classrooms. With a mixture of plain flour and water to make glue, coloured paper in various shapes and sizes was transformed into Chinese lanterns, bells and paper chains.

At lunchtime, Tommy and Tiny were idling their time away in the playground.

Tommy kicked a stone, 'I'm bored.'

'Let's take the afternoon off and go to that toyshop in the High Street. We could get some ideas of what to ask Father Christmas for.'

'Can't. I've already done my letter. I did it at half term.'

'But I haven't done mine yet.'

Tommy liked the idea of skipping off school, 'Besides, we'd get into trouble for playing truant.'

Laughing, Tiny shook his head, the music teacher was crossing the playground, 'Look! It's Miss Beck! She's soft. I bet we could get round her OK.' He grabbed his pal's arm and pulled it round his shoulder. 'Hang on to me, and limp — like you're in a lot of pain.'

'Miss, Miss.'

The worried music teacher hurried towards them.

'Miss, Tommy's twisted his ankle. Miss.'

'Owch!' Tommy felt Tiny's elbow dig into his ribs and the penny dropped. 'It really hurts, Miss.'

'I suppose we'd better be safe than sorry. Your ankle, you say?'

'Yes, Miss. It hurts something awful.'

'Oh dear . . . and today of all days when the Headmaster is away.'

'I could take him home, Miss.'

'Yes, and then his mother can decide what to do!' Never good in a crisis, the gentle spinster was relieved to have a solution presented to her.

'Ooow, it's really painful, Miss.'

Tiny nudged his 'injured' accomplice, 'Don't overdo it, she'll smell a rat or send for help.'

'Are you sure you can manage?'

'Don't you worry, Miss. It isn't far.'

'O.K, run along now or should I say hop-it?' And with a nervous laugh, 'I'll let everyone know where you are.'

As soon as they were out of the school gates, and out of sight, the two friends ran off to the High Street, laughing and congratulating themselves on a well carried out con.

⋆　⋆　⋆

They were soon looking around the crowded toyshop, wide eyed with excitement. 'I think I'll ask Father Christmas for some of these.'

Tommy laughed, 'You'll be lucky!'

'Why?'

Tommy shook his head, ''Cos my mum said you can only have one big present. Only people in posh houses get lots of really expensive presents. We're in a council flat so we're at the bottom of Santa's list anyway!'

His friend looked distraught, 'That's not fair.'

'Well in the war we got nuffin!'

51

They wandered around Bents's with ever widening grins. How on earth was anyone child supposed to choose ONE toy! And then ... there before their eyes was a dazzling display of Dinky toys. 'Cor, just look at that. I bet they've got every Dinky that was ever made.'

'Yeah,' Tommy agreed. 'Looks like the whole range to me.'

Picking up a police car and a taxi they raced them along the counter.

An annoyed young assistant behind the counter reprimanded them, 'If you're not buying, please don't touch!'

Tommy looked apologetic, 'Sorry, Miss, we were only playing.'

Her expression softened and swiftly changed to a smile, 'We've had a lot of shoplifting lately, and this morning we even had a couple of boxes of toy cars snatched from the delivery van, so I have to be very strict.'

The boys looked at the cars covetously, 'How much?' She told him, and he pulled a face, 'No chance, I'll ask Father Christmas for some.'

The girl smiled knowingly as she put the cars back on display. Tommy grabbed Tiny by the sleeve and pulled him towards the exit, 'I know, let's go to the market and see what toys they have there.'

★   ★   ★

Church Street Market was alive with people; the general babble could be heard a street away. Outside, Christmas shoppers laden down with bags and parcels were queuing at the bus stop or struggling down the road.

All was hustle and bustle. Above the noise costermongers shouted raucously, as they tried to clear their stalls of goods cleverly displayed in the most decorative manner. It did not take the boys long to find the toy stall, where a tough unshaven man was waving a toy racing car in his hand. 'Dinky toys half price. Get 'em while you can!'

'We still can't afford them at that price.' Tiny muttered to Tommy who was examining a police car on the stall.

'Oi, put that down, you can look, but don't touch.' The costermonger's shout cut through the noise of the mingling crowd.

'Don't worry, mate, we are going to ask Father Christmas for some.'

The stallholder burst out laughing. 'Father Christmas? You don't still believe in Father Christmas, do you?'

'Clear off, you ragamuffins!'

The two boys were dumbstruck, 'What d'yer mean? No Father Christmas?'

Tommy felt outraged, angry and sad. 'We don't care what you say. Our Mums say he's real and they'd never lie to us. It's just that he's having a hard time, 'cos of the war.'

'Yeah, my Mum says she hopes he's got more money than what she has or none of us'll get very much,' Tiny agreed. 'Anyway I bet you nicked them cars and that's why they're cheap!'

The market trader's attitude abruptly changed and red faced with anger he shook his fist at the boys, 'Clear off, you ragamuffins before I give you some of this!'

Running through the crowd in the cold afternoon air Tommy shivered, 'Let's go back to Bents's Toyshop, at least it's warmer there.'

★ ★ ★

Much to the annoyance of the shop assistants, they wandered through the busy store picking up and playing with guns and other toys. Eventually they found themselves back amongst the Dinky toys.

'Hello again.' the assistant greeted them, 'Have you found some more money?'

Tommy looked sad, 'Nah Miss, we've been down Church St. Market. A barro' boy down there was selling dinky toys at half price. He was really nasty. I reckon he's the one what stole from your van.'

'The Dinky toys were definitely half price were they?'

'Yes, Miss.'

'It does seem suspicious. I'll tell the manager. He'll find out if they're the ones stolen from us or not. I'll just take your name and address, you never know there may be a reward.'

The boy's faces lit up. 'That would be great!'

'I've got all your details. I'd better take a note of the time you were there.'

'Time?' Tiny mused.

'TIME! The school bell's probably gone by now we've got to leg it.'

Tiny left Tommy at his house. 'What about Shirley? I always bring her home.'

'I'll get her, you can't go, you're supposed to be injured. And don't forget to limp!'

Tiny ran off to the school gates where Shirley was waiting anxiously. 'Where's Tommy. What have you two been up to?'

Flustered, Tiny hesitated before answering, 'He had an accident at school and I had to take him home.'

Shirley eyed him with suspicious, 'I've been here ages.'

'Come on, I'll take you home.'

Later that afternoon the family were sitting at the kitchen table having their tea when there was a heavy knock at the door. Rose automatically got up to see who it was. Tommy could hear whispered conversations and then his mother entered the kitchen with a policeman.

'Why weren't you at school this afternoon?'

The colour drained from Tommy's face; he guiltily remained silent. Arthur leaned threateningly across the table, 'Answer yer mother.'

'I never believed him. He forgot which leg to limp with, for one thing.'

Tommy didn't know what to say. He glowered at his sister and then gabbled out everything in one breath, ending hopefully with, 'I'm sorry, Mum, Dad.'

An angry father rose to his feet, 'How many times have you done something like this before, lad?'

'This was the first time honest, Dad.'

Arthur slowly calmed down, 'Make it the last time, lad or you'll feel the back of my hand.'

The policeman intervened, 'Calm down, sir, the toyshop are very grateful to your son and his friend because, acting on their information, we caught a thief that we have been after for some time.'

Rose smiled, 'Yes and if they go into the shop tomorrow they can pick out a Dinky toy each as a reward.'

'Can we?' Tommy's heart was racing with all the excitement.

He was soon brought down to earth by his father, 'This doesn't excuse missing school so it's an early night for you. And tomorrow you'll have to apologise, and admit to your teacher you lied about hurting your leg.'

'But Dad, I'll get detention or even the cane!' Arthur shook his head, 'That's life, son. You'll probably be lucky enough to get away with it once they hear the full story, but whatever happens you've got to learn to be honest! Cheats never prosper.'

5

Junior Gardeners

Tommy was on a platform at Euston Railway Station, attached to his lapel was a label stating his name and destination, Wolverhampton. Rose held her frightened child close to her. 'It's for the best, son. It's too dangerous here. You'll see there will be lot's of other children being evacuated, too.'

Tommy was too terrified to ask what 'evacuated' meant, even though she was cheerfully hugging and kissing him. 'It's all right, you'll be coming home when it's safe.' As long as his mother was there with him he felt comforted.

Then the guard shouted, 'All aboard! Hurry along, now.'

His mother hurriedly lifted him into the train crowded with other tearful children. Some of them had buckets and spades. His mother had said nothing about going to the seaside.

'Are we going to the seaside, Mum?'

'No, son.' Some mothers had told their children nice tales to make the parting easier.

59

Rose couldn't bring herself to lie to her son. Better he be told the truth than he lost his faith in her.

The carriage door closed. His heart beat faster. Panic stricken, he leant out of the carriage window and cried, 'Mummy, Mummy, I don't wanna go!'

Rose, trying to hold back her own tears, was blowing him kisses shouting, 'It'll be all right, Tommy.'

'Why can't I stay. Tiny isn't going. His Mum isn't getting rid of him.'

What could his mother find to say to her terrified child?

'What if them Germans were to bomb the school, Tommy. It don't bear thinking about.'

He knew his mother would not change her mind. It didn't matter what he said, she thought she was doing the best thing. But, tears were streaming down his cheeks. His only solace being the shared grief of the other children: their faces as tear stained as his own.

The train gradually got up steam and slowly chugged out of the station, his mother's figure became smaller and smaller until she disappeared into the distance . . .

Rose heard Tommy's scream and rushed into his room. Taking him into her arms, she

60

cooed, 'It's all right son, it's only a dream.'

He looked around and remembered: it was 1948 and he was safe in his bed with his mother there to soothe his troubled mind. The nightmares were less frequent and the doctor had said they would slowly disappear as the years went by.

'You start your summer holidays today, Tommy.' Rose laughed at him as he wriggled free from the cuddle he had, up to then, enjoyed.

'Move over, Mum. Tiny and I are going to Finchley Road this morning.'

'Poking around the old bomb sites, I bet.' She wagged a finger in mock anger, 'You be careful. Them places make dangerous playgrounds.' The boys had been there many times before, but they still had quite a few to investigate.

Tommy was enjoying his breakfast when he saw his mother approaching with a spoon in one hand and a bottle in the other. 'Oh, no, Mum . . . Must I?'

'Yes.' Pouring a tablespoon full of liquid paraffin she ordered, 'Open wide!'

'It tastes disgusting.'

Shirley was enjoying her brother's discomfort, as he anticipated the evil taste to come. 'You should have thought of that before you had your toast and marmalade. You know

Mum makes us have it every Monday morning.'

Tommy pulled a face, 'Ugh! That was 'orrible!'

His mother laughed, 'Don't worry, it'll keep you regular! Now here's a couple of bob, I'll be out all day so you'll have to get some pie and pop, or something, from the chippie.'

'Where are you going then?' His mother, who had already been up several hours, getting the family up and her husband off to work, was getting agitated. 'Look I've got a very busy day. After taking your sister round to your Auntie Maude's, I'm off to work. Then I've got to collect Shirley and go shopping, so make yourself scarce!'

Tommy smiled. He was looking forward to his day out with Tiny. 'At least I won't have to put up with her. Aunt Maud'll sort her out.'

'Beast!'

★   ★   ★

As arranged Tiny was there on the corner waiting, 'All right, Tom,' he yelled.

'Yeah, I don't have to go home for ages, look I've got some dinner money.'

Tiny was pleased, 'So have I, ain't it great!'

Tommy laughed, 'Come on, I'll race you to

62

the tube station.' They ran off in the direction of Finchley Road only stopping for breath at St. Johns Wood Tube Station.

Walking up Finchley Road they entered the first derelict Victorian house they came across. Climbing up dusty, rickety, old stairs they made their way to the roof and climbed out: carefully avoiding the holes and loose tiles. Looking down from the sloping roof they watched the people below passing by, and shouted out anything that came into their heads, like, 'Look out' and, 'Oi Baldy'. And then laughed when their bewildered victims looked around, unable to see who was shouting at them.

They were soon bored, and climbed back into the derelict building, treading carefully over broken floorboards and down staircases, smashed by fallen masonry from the roof.

'Wonder what's in the back garden. Bit overgrown, but there might be something worth having.'

But there were just some old weeds, stinging nettles and an old crab apple tree. Tiny was disappointed, 'It's a pity there isn't anything growing, I bet this was lovely before it was bombed.'

Tommy examined what, at first, he thought were nettles. He pinched a leaf between his fingers and smelled its juice. 'Over here. It's

63

mint! We could take some of this home, my Mum uses it on the meat sometimes.'

'Yeah, there's nothing else we can take home, not even flowers.'

Tommy's face lit up like a beacon, he had a brainwave, 'Let's get some seeds and grow something ourselves.'

'Where can we get some seeds?'

'At a shop stupid! We can use our dinner money. We'll still have enough for some fish and chips, or something.'

'Great, we can plant some vegetables and take them home when they've grown.'

They rushed back through the house and out the front door, 'This way, there's a gardening shop in St John's Wood High St.'

* * *

Tommy took a packet of cabbage seeds from the seed stand and went up to the counter to pay.

His pal was puzzled, 'We'll need more than a packet of cabbage seeds, won't we?'

Tommy smiled, 'Don't worry, I have an idea.'

The grey haired shopkeeper behind the counter held out his hand, 'That'll be thruppence, young man please.'

Tommy gave him the money and the boys

made their way back to the house in Finchley Road.

They had found an old piece of wood and sharp pointed stones, and working hard they managed to pull up a patch of weeds and till some ground.

Tommy cursed, 'I'll be glad when I get long trousers. These nettles are hot.'

'My Mum says I can have some next year.'

'Me, too. Seems to me next year never comes.' He scratched his legs.

'Don't scratch at your legs like that, it'll make 'em itch worse than ever.'

'I can't help it. Don't just stand there gawping. Help me find a dock leaf.'

Within a few minutes the young herbalists had found the necessary medication, rubbed the large green and red leaves until they released the soothing juice, and squeezed it onto the bright red rash.

'Cor! That's better.'

'Open the packet let's see how many we've got. Here give it to me.' Tiny was getting impatient, carefully he opened the top and peered inside. 'Ain't they small.'

'Be careful or they'll all fall out.'

'What do we do with 'em?'

'Read what it says on the back.'

The instructions were read and the seeds planted accordingly.

'Don't we have to water them in?'

'Where can we get some water?'

Tiny thought for a minute, 'I know, I'm dying for a pee!' and without another word he undid his trousers and relieved himself over their brand new gardening plot.

'Are you sure that's O.K?'

''Course it is, now is that all we're going to plant?'

'No, look,' Tommy waved the empty packet of seeds, and bent down to pick up several very small bits of grit and stone. These he put in the packet and very carefully sealed it up again. 'Come on, back to the shop!' He grabbed his friend's arm and off they went to St John's Wood High St.

★　★　★

Re-entering the gardening shop Tommy headed straight for the grey haired man that had served him previously and waved the packet of seeds at him, 'Can I change these please, mister?' Looking very sorrowful, 'I made a mistake, my Dad wanted carrot seeds.'

The shopkeeper sighed wearily and looked

over his glasses, 'Don't worry, sonny.' He took the packet and put it back into the cabbage section. 'Here you are, a good cropping carrot.'

Tiny looked on astonished.

Outside the shop they both ran off, laughing, back to their private little vegetable patch in Finchley Rd, stopping only to buy some fish and chips.

'There you are!' said Tommy triumphantly, 'we'll plant these and keep the packet, and do the same thing again.'

Tiny shook his head, 'Will he fall for it a second time?'

Tommy looked confident, 'Why not?'

Kneeling down, he planted several rows of carrot seeds and covered them with soil. Keeping the packet open he filled it with small stones, and sealed it. A spot of rain splashed onto his cheek. The sky was cloudy and dark. He held his hand out to confirm it was actually raining and smiled, 'At least we won't need your wee willie watering can.' And, giggling, they both ran into the derelict house.

After a heavy shower the rain soon stopped, and Tommy waved the packet of seeds. 'Let's go and swop these!'

★ ★ ★

As they approached the gardening shop they could hear a voice raised in anger.

'What's all that about, Tiny?'

'Dunno.'

Quietly they crept through the shop door to see what all the excitement was all about. An angry, red-faced customer slapped something down on the counter, 'Look there were no seeds in the packet, just these little stones.'

The shopkeeper looked shocked, 'I'm sorry, Mr. Higgs, I can't understand it.' And then his gaze fixed on the two boys who had about turned, as if to make a hasty exit, and immediately he recognised the culprits. 'It's them, quick grab them.' In an instant the irate customer turned round and had them by the scruff of their necks.

The shopkeeper came round the counter; 'I changed those seeds for you this morning, didn't I?'

An embarrassed Tommy stuttered, 'Yeh, we wanted some more seeds for our secret garden. We're really sorry, mister!'

Mr. Higgs, holding them, looked sympathetic, 'Are you interested in gardening?'

The boys looked at each, 'Yeah.'

'Not 'alf!'

'We've just started, but only had enough money for one packet of seeds.'

The somewhat calmer customer smiled

and shook his head, 'Well then, you should know that although oak trees from little acorns grow, nothing grows from little stones. As much as I admire your enterprise I can't agree with what you've done, so how shall we punish you? Either I take you to your parents and tell them what you've done or you can come down to my allotment at Townsend Cottages and do a very special job for me!'

The boys were nodding their heads vigorously, 'Anything, mister, but don't tell our parents please!'

The shopkeeper shook his head; 'I'd call the police if it was up to me.' Mr. Higgs' weather beaten face broke into a broad smile and winked, 'No, I've a very special job for them. It will be worth paying for another packet of seeds to get this job done!' So saying he handed over the money in exchange for some more seeds and marched the two boys out of the shop.

Half of the allotment was very tidy and organised, with a shed and some runner beans growing up sticks by the side of a fence. There were a few neat rows of young plants signposted with empty seed packets to indicate what was growing in each row. The other half looked barren, with just turned over earth and nothing planted there.

Mr. Higgs went into the shed and came out

Digging out the dung!

with two spades and a bottle of beer; he took a mouthful of beer and handed the tools to the boys. With beer dripping from his straggly moustache he pointed to a container at the far end of the allotment, 'See that box, I want you to empty it. Shovel it all out onto that turned over earth and then rake it in all over. Once you've done that you can go. O.K lads?'

As the boys approached the container they noticed a nasty smell that got stronger and stronger. Tiny pulled a face 'Ugh! What's that?'

Tommy opened the box to be enveloped in the rancid, pungent smell of manure. Gingerly they started digging out the dung and putting it on the turned-over soil.

Mr. Higgs, hands on hips, looked on, 'Go on, put your backs into it. I'm lucky to get that from the milkman's horse. He passes my house every morning and I nip out with a shovel and bucket. That's how I manage to grow the best vegetables in the area.'

The boys started working a lot quicker, but less carefully, bits of manure fell into their shoes and socks. Eventually the box was empty. Getting a couple of rakes from the shed the boys systematically raked the manure into the turned over earth.

Holding another bottle of beer, Mr. Higgs came over to inspect the area. 'Well done lads, you can go now. I hope you've learned your lesson.'

★ ★ ★

Hot, bothered and smelly, the two boys made their way back to the derelict house in Finchley Road just as it started to rain again. 'That was hard work. It was alright for him drinking beer all the time, but I'm hot, thirsty and ache all over.'

Tommy muttered, 'Let's shelter in the house out of the rain, it's too early to go home.'

His friend looked despondent, 'Yeah, it's boring at home ain't it?'

Tommy nodded in agreement, 'What do your Mum and Dad talk about?'

Tiny put his head in his hands and looked puzzled, 'I dunno, I don't understand a lot of it, it's all politics and that . . . The other night they were all excited about this new National 'elf Service thing, talked about it all night.'

Tommy looked at him as though he knew exactly what he meant, 'I know! My mum belongs to the Labour Party. She goes to meetings and everything! When that Lady Lucan comes round selling the Labour Life they're talking for ages.'

He looked exasperated before continuing,

72

'And when my Mum and Dad turn the wireless on to listen to the news, they have a great big discussion about parliament and fings, sometimes it turns into an argument and I'm trying to listen to the latest Olympic news.'

Tiny's face lit up, 'Yeah, ain't that Zatopek good? I saw him on the news when my Dad took me to the flicks last week. He can 'arf run!'

'What your Dad?'

'No you idiot! Zatopek. And that Fanny Blankers something from Holland cor, she's lightning!'

Tommy looked at him enviously, 'You jammy sod, my Dad never takes me to the flicks.' Then as an afterthought, 'He's normally home too late. He just lights the fire, if it's cold, and flops into his armchair until his dinner's ready.'

'My Dad works in the estate agents as a clerk near where we live, so he's always home just after six, and he likes all sorts of sport.'

Tommy groaned, 'My dad only likes horse racing and that's because he has a shilling each way on something, mind you, he likes Tommy Handley so he lets me listen to ITMA.'

They both started to sing, 'It's that man again'.

Tiny remembered, 'My Mum and Dad like Victor Sylvester and his orchestra.'

Tommy grinned, 'My Mum jokes with my Dad that he's got Victor Sylvester trousers 'cos there's plenty of ballroom!'

His friend roared with laughter, 'They are a bit baggy.'

A shaft of sunlight penetrated the clouds and it stopped raining, 'I wonder what the time is. Let's climb up on the roof again and look at the church clock.'

The two boys were soon up on the roof, where they could see the church clock, a few hundred yards down the road. It was just after four o'clock. Tommy thought for a moment 'I'll have to go home now.'

Tiny nodded sadly, adding proudly, 'O.K., but lets get some mint from OUR garden first.'

'Yeah, our SECRET garden,' Tommy emphasised. 'Don't tell anyone about it will you?'

''Course not.'

★   ★   ★

Halfway home the heavens opened and, although the two boys ran as fast as they could they couldn't avoid getting soaked to the skin. 'See you tomorrow,' Tommy shouted as he reached his front door.

His friend shouted something incomprehensible in reply and continued running down the street towards home.

Tommy knew his mother was in: the key wasn't under the mat. He rang the bell and shouted through the letterbox, 'I'm home, Mum. Let me in.'

Rose answered the door, 'Look at the state of you! You're like a drowned rat! You'll catch yer death!' She sniffed the air, 'And what's that 'orrible smell?'

Her son looked so sad and apologetic, 'Nothing, Mum. Honest.' Quickly changing the subject, 'Look, I've got you some mint.' And wiping his feet on the doormat, he handed his mother a soaking wet bedraggled bunch of mint as though it was the loveliest bouquet of flowers imaginable.

Rose smiled, her anger subsided and mellowed, she ushered her son inside the front door. 'Stay there while I put the mint away.' Then, as an afterthought, she added, 'Get undressed and I'll get a towel to dry you.'

Tommy was slowly pulling off his wet clothes when his sister Shirley came out of her bedroom, and giggled as he hid behind the coat stand trying to take off his underpants.

His mother returned with a nice big towel, 'Get back in your bedroom, my girl.'

She wrapped the towel around her naked son, 'Now go and have a nice hot bath before your father gets home.'

Rose picked up the discarded clothes, sniffed and grimaced in disgust, 'Ugh! God knows what you've been doing. These are going in the wash they smell 'orrible! You'll really be for it my boy if you ever come home smelling like this again.'

Unknown to his mother, Tommy hadn't heard her above the sound of the running water. His mind was elsewhere as already he was thinking of tomorrow morning, when he would get the old coal shovel and bucket from the shed, and follow the milkman's horse to collect some manure for their secret garden. Then in a few months time he would really surprise her by bringing home some vegetables as nice as those Mr. Higgs grows, wouldn't she be pleased.

6

We're All Going To The Zoo

Tommy, his mother, older sister Pamela and brother Freddie were struggling up Church Street. They had just left the air raid shelter. Tommy was holding his mother's hand tightly: as though his very life depended on it. If she let him go would he ever find her again. She was pulling him along, faster than his little legs wanted to go. 'Mummy, my legs ache.'

'Stop moaning and get a move on!'

He couldn't see. He couldn't breathe properly. 'You're going too fast.'

His head still hurt from the noise. Even the ground in the shelter had been shaken. And he'd never seen the grownups so frightened before.

'Why were the bangs so loud, Mummy?'

His mother gripped his hand harder and jerked him along.

'Mummy, you're hurting my hand.'

'Oh, do shut up,' she shouted. Who was this woman. His mother never shouted.

'Don't be such a baby!' Pamela grabbed his other hand and dragged him along even faster.

His only relief were the red-hot tears that washed the dust out of his burning eyes, leaving rivulets in the dust lingering on his cheeks.

And then they were there . . . But in place where their house should have been was a big pile of broken bricks. And Granddad, with some other people, was desperately pulling brick after brick off the top of the debris.

His mother called out, 'Dad!

And his Granddad turned. He was crying and shouting at the same time, 'Thank God! I thought you were all in there.'

Tommy had never seen his Granddad cry. Then Tommy was crying out louder and louder, 'Mummy, Mummy where's Tootsie . . .?

Rose came into the bedroom comforting him with a cup of tea, 'What was it this time?'

Her young son had tears in his eyes, 'Remember when I was very little, and our house got bombed. And my kitten, Tootsie was killed!'

His mother nodded sadly. She remembered only too well. She would never forget that walk back to Lisson Grove from the underground shelter. It was 1941; Arthur was away in the Army. She was on her own with the children.

A few hours earlier, huddled together, they had heard some terrible explosions. No one could sleep, everyone's imagination ran riot, fearing the worst. The air raid was much too close for comfort.

Did they have homes to go back to?

Did all their friends and relatives get to the safety of the shelters?

Every step back to Lisson Grove was sheer torture. And it was hard to breathe; the air was full of dust and blankets of smoke hung stung their eyes. The children were scared and so was she.

She remembered his continual grizzling and how short tempered she had been, tugging him every inch of the way home.

Home! That was a joke. The memory of the sight that greeted them, when they eventually got back to the Grove, still brought tears to her eyes. Through the smoke and debris all she could see was their house, reduced to a pile of rubble and her father and some of their friends tearing into the broken bricks with their bare hands, frantically searching . . .

They had lost everything.

★ ★ ★

'There, there, you're all right now.' To cheer him up, she reminded him, 'At least there's no school today.'

Tommy dried his eyes and smiled, 'Yeah, me and Tiny are going to bunk into the Zoo.'

Rose pretended she hadn't heard. Boys will be boys. 'Come on, drink that tea and get out of bed.' She opened the curtains to let the bright sunshine stream into the bedroom. 'I've got an interview today for a new job.'

Tommy was curious, 'Who with?'

His mother smiled, 'With Mrs. Flanagan! You know Bud Flanagan's wife.'

Her son looked proud, he had heard Bud Flanagan on the wireless and even seen him in the newspapers. 'Where does he live, then?'

'Not far from your Auntie Maude; in that little house around the corner from the police station. It's quite handy 'cos I can drop Shirley off at yer Auntie's when I go.'

Tommy jumped out of bed and headed for the bathroom.

While his mother was getting herself and Shirley ready, Tommy ate his breakfast as quickly as he could.

'Right, we're off now! I'll leave the key under the mat as usual.'

He left home and raced down the road; excited at the prospect of his Mum working for someone really famous, he couldn't wait to tell Tiny.

★ ★ ★

'Guess what!' Tommy exclaimed excitedly, 'My mother might be cleaning for Bud Flanagan soon!'

Tony was impressed. 'What? Flanagan and Allen?' he asked open mouthed.

As they headed for Regents Park they were talking continuously about Tommy's mother and whether she would get her new job. Occasionally they broke into singing, 'Underneath the Arches, I dream my dreams away.'

They entered the park from Charlbert Street, by the banks of the Regent Canal, known locally as 'the slips'. The canal was known as 'the cut'. Tommy pointed past the leafy tress and down the banks of 'the slips.' 'Come on, let's see if we can find any money.'

His pal looked at him in surprise, 'What d'you mean?'

Looking up to the heavens Tommy asked superiorly, 'Don't you know anyfing! The airmen stationed at Bentinck Close take the local girls over here at night for their kissing and cuddling, and sometimes coins fall out of their pockets.'

They ran down the banks to the canal towpath and were soon searching through the long grass. Tiny was the first to find silver, 'I've found two bob!'

Tommy's fingers divided the undergrowth meticulously as he frantically peered through the vegetation, but search as he may he was disappointed. He couldn't find anything.

Leaving 'the slips', they walked across the bridge. Tommy pointed down at the dark murky waters of the canal, 'D'you remember last summer when we went fishing? We made some rods out of sticks, string and safety pins, but then it got so hot we ended up swimming in our underpants?'

Tiny's friend nodded, 'Do I? I was swinging from that rope under the bridge doing my Tarzan call when that park keeper came along.'

'You ran away, like Cheetah the monkey, when he chased you.'

'At least I managed to grab my clothes and get away.'

Tommy was indignant, 'Well I was still in the water! I didn't stand a chance. I had to put my clothes back on while I was still soaking wet.'

'Didn't you have to go to the cop shop?'

'Nah! He threatened to take me to the police station, but in the end he just took me home and told my Mum. She went potty, reckoned we could catch polio swimming in 'the cut'. What with the water rats and all sorts of rubbish that's been dumped in there.'

His accomplice shrugged his shoulders, 'Well, we didn't catch anything, did we? Not even a stickleback.' Then laughed, 'Race you to the Zoo.'

★ ★ ★

The two boys were soon running through the park until they came to the railings surrounding The London Zoo. They walked along until they found the bent railing where they knew from past experiences they could squeeze through.

Once inside they made their way to the Parrot House where they spent ages trying to teach the parrots rude words and giggling like girls when they succeeded.

They had great fun teasing the monkeys, and Tommy was helpless with laughter when Tiny got too near the bars and a monkey sprayed him. 'He's pee'd all over me.'

'Let's go the Aquarium.'

'Then the Reptile House.'

A crowd of people were gathered around the barriers throwing coins in at the crocodiles. 'Look at all that money on the crocodiles backs, I wonder if anyone has ever tried to snatch it from them?'

Tiny shook his head, 'I doubt it, they'd get their arm bitten off.'

'I suppose so, just like that nasty bloke in the Tarzan film we saw last Saturday!'

'Why do people throw money at the crocs anyway? Are they like a wishing well or summat?'

'Nah, I don't fink so, it's probably 'cos they lie so still in the water that people throw coins to see if they can make them move. They look so sleepy yet our teacher told us that when they are on land they can outrun a man!'

'What do you think the Zoo does with all the money?'

'I dunno, do I!' Tommy then laughed, 'I expect they leave it there as long as possible. It's a lot safer than the bank! Lets go and have something to eat, we've got our dinner money and that two bob you found in the slips.'

Tiny agreement, 'Yeah, we can afford some ice creams as well.'

After bread rolls and ice cream they wandered through the crowds. Although they had been to the Zoo several times, they were still in awe of all the wild animals that, not long ago, they had only seen at the flicks or in schoolbooks.

Tommy pointed at some giraffes, 'Look at the size of them. They're the tallest animals in the world.'

'I feel sorry for 'em.'

'Don't be silly, anyway they are safer in here 'cos they get killed and eaten by lions in the wild.'

'Nah,' Tiny empathised, 'I mean I know what it's like for people to stare at you just because you're tall.'

Tommy grinned, 'Don't be silly, you're not that tall.' Then laughed, 'If you had a neck like that then even I'd take the mickey!'

Tiny smiled weakly, 'You know what I mean. Come on, let's go and see the Elephants.'

Tommy happily agreed, 'Yeah, we can imagine we're Sabu the Elephant Boy and they are all our elephants.'

'It's a pity we can't ride them.'

'It must be great to be up there pulling his ears to change direction. Cor, imagine riding one all the way home!'

Excitedly, Tiny headed for the Elephant House, but Tommy was quiet and thoughtful, 'I know, after we've seen the elephants let's go down to where the Shetland ponies are.'

'Why? They're not very interesting!'

'If we can't ride an elephant, we could try and ride a pony!'

'Don't be silly.'

But Tommy was adamant, 'You'll see!'

'Don't you want to see the elephants, then?'

Tommy shrugged his shoulders, 'I can't wait to see the Shetland ponies. There's never many people down there. We could get over the fence and have a ride.'

Tiny was doubtful, 'I don't know.'

'Come on, I'll race you,' Tommy pulled him away by his wrist. They ran through the Zoo until they arrived at a fenced off compound by the side of 'the cut'. 'See, there's no one around.'

Still struggling for breath, Tiny didn't seem so pleased. Breathlessly he waved at the fence, 'I'm not going to climb over there.'

'Well, you can help me over, then!'

'It's a bit dodgy.'

'Come on scaredy cat. I'm going to ride that pony over there.' Tommy pointed to the smallest pony in sight. Reluctantly Tiny linked his hands together and lifted his friend up and over the wire fencing.

Tommy fell down the other side. His coat caught the wire, tearing his sleeve and scratching his hand. Not wanting to frighten the pony, he approached very slowly. He patted the pony's side to reassure it, and then quickly mounted, just like he'd seen his hero Roy Rogers jump on Trigger at the flicks. But the pony wasn't as friendly as Trigger. Like a bucking bronco, the pony sped towards the fence at the bottom of the slope by the canal.

Tiny watched in horror as the pony kicked his hind legs in the air and threw Tommy over the fence and into the cut. As if in slow motion, Tommy landed with a big splash, to reappear and swim to the towpath. He crawled onto the street-side bank and stood, dripping wet. Determined not to show how foolish and scared he felt, he punched the air with his fist and shouted across to his pal, 'Ride 'em cowboy,' and laughed out loud.

Tiny shook his head, 'You're crazy! Stay there, I'm coming out,' and headed for the Zoo's exit.

★ ★ ★

Coming out of the Zoo into Prince Albert Road Tiny ran down to the slips and met a very soggy Tommy walking up the bank. 'What's your Mum going to say?'

'You could say there was a really bad thunderstorm at the Zoo!' Tommy thought for a moment, 'I dunno, I'll say we went on the boats at Regents Park Lake and splashed each other with the oars.' Then with a wicked smile, 'Or I could say you pushed me in.'

Tiny panicked for a moment, 'Thanks very much!'

'Just joking!' He hid behind a tree, stripped to the waist trying to wring his shirt and jacket out. 'At least the sun's shining.' He hung them on a branch, and removed his short trousers and pants and tried to squeeze

'How do I look now?'

as much water out of them as he could. Once he was satisfied that he had removed as much water from his clothing as possible he dressed himself, 'How do I look now?'

Tiny looked him up and down, 'Like you've gone through a mangle backwards, I've never seen so many creases.'

Tommy was disappointed, 'Oh well, let's go home and face the music.'

The two boys walked home in silence. As they parted company Tiny waved goodbye, 'Best of luck, see you tomorrow.'

★　★　★

Tommy nodded and made his way to his flat. The key wasn't under the mat so he knocked at the door and shouted through the letterbox as usual. His mother answered the door with a big happy smile on her face. Her mood immediately changed to anger when she looked at her son. 'What on earth . . . ?' her voice trailed off despairingly. 'What have you been up to now?' Rose pulled Tommy inside, 'Look at the state of you. You're soaking wet.'

Her son was near to tears, 'I'm sorry, Mum.' He looked at her apologetically, 'After we went to the zoo we were messing about on the boats at the park, splashing each other and that.'

Without warning Shirley came running out of her bedroom shouting, 'I bet you're telling fibs. Tommy's telling fibs!'

Her brother glared at her. He hated his little sister sometimes. Rose looked at him disbelievingly, 'As long as you haven't been swimming in that canal again!'

Dragging him along the passage, with Shirley laughing out loud in pursuit, Rose pointed to the bathroom, 'Get those wet things off and jump in a hot bath! Put your things in the kitchen sink and I'll wash them later with everything else. I was in such a good mood as well, I got that job with Bud Flanagan, now look at me. Can't you just go out one day without getting into a mess?'

Tommy just wanted to get into the hot bath and stay there forever. As he slowly shut the bathroom door he heard his mother say, 'You haven't heard the last of this, my boy. Wait til your father comes home you'll be for it! And I've got some news just for you as well, which you won't like, I'm sure!'

★   ★   ★

Later that evening Tommy heard his father's key in the door and quickly disappeared to his bedroom. Words were muttered between his mother and father and then his father's

90

voice bellowed, 'Come out of your bedroom, Tommy!'

Sheepishly he came out and faced his parents. Still in his postman's uniform and bicycle clips, red faced with anger, his father shouted, 'What have you been up to today?' Tommy repeated the story he had told his mother.

Arthur looked at him, exasperated, 'I hope you are telling the truth, if I find out you're lying you'll be laughing on the other side of your face, my boy. Behave yourself and stop giving your mother grief, we're both out there working trying to give you kids a better life. If you keep messing us about you'll have to stay in and look after your sister. It'll give Auntie Maud a break.' Tommy was relieved to get off so lightly, although the thought of being stuck with his sister all day filled him with horror. 'O.K, Dad, I'm sorry.'

Rose Harris, feeling sorry for her son, changed the subject, 'I got that job at Bud Flanagan's.'

Arthur was pleased, 'Brilliant, at least that's good news.'

His wife smiled, 'I've also got some news for Tommy, I think it's about time you earned your keep, my lad. There's a paperboy wanted at Pike's, the newsagents. I called in there and said you'll look in tomorrow and if he likes you, the job's yours.'

Tommy was dumbfounded, 'I'll have to get up early!'

His mother laughed, 'It's about time, too, it's good pay. Seven and sixpence a week. Out of that you can give me half a crown and I can buy Co-op stamps to put towards your clothes. Every little helps, as the old lady said when she piddled in the sea.' Tommy didn't laugh. 'Then you can buy your own comics. And pay for your Saturday morning pictures. You've got to learn money don't grow on trees, son.' Tommy felt life was conspiring against him.

That night he lay in bed thinking about tomorrow. It was bad enough going to school, but he wasn't looking forward to doing a paper round beforehand. Ten years old, and he was starting work.

He tried to be positive and look on the bright side. At least he would have his own money. Five shillings a week! It seemed a fortune to him, but he knew deep down his parents wouldn't let him spend it on anything he liked. Already they had told him he had to pay out for his own comics and flicks. What else would they think of?

7

Cricket, Lovely Cricket

Tommy stood in the school's main hall in the midst of a group of other six year olds. Everyone was quiet and sad. He looked around for his special friends. Where were Maureen Corby and her brother Tony?

His attention was drawn to a seemingly distant voice. The head master was addressing them, 'I have some very bad news for you all. You all heard the air raid last night and you were probably all down the air raid shelter while it was going on. Well I'm afraid some families didn't manage to get to the shelter in time and . . .'

Tommy looked up and was deeply shocked. This man for whom every child and teacher in the school held deep respect, even fear; this man, who was a tower of strength for the whole community, had tears in his eyes. Gaining control of his faltering voice the Headmaster announced, 'Maureen and Tony Corby's house was bombed and all the family were killed . . . '
And unable to continue, he unashamedly

let the tears stream down his cheeks.

The whole school was shocked into silence as the news was gradually taken in by all the children. Tommy felt hot tears burn his eyes and trickle down his face. He put his hands over his eyes, but couldn't prevent the tears running through his fingers as they turned to a flood. And the sobbing in the hall grew louder and louder . . .

Tommy woke up, his head on a pillow wet from the tears. Wiping his eyes he was overjoyed to find himself back in 1948, and it was his school's summer holiday. Occasionally, he still thought of Maureen Corby, especially when he passed the building site where her family lived. Tommy liked to believe that Maureen and her brother were looking down on the world today, with all the other children who perished in the war. His mother came into the bedroom with a cup of tea and noticed the damp pillow, 'You been crying?

'I was dreaming about Maureen and Tony.'

His mother looked sorrowful as she gathered him in her arms, 'There, there, son, it's all over now.'

Tommy forced a smile and he looked up at her, 'D'yer remember a few weeks later when we saw a coffin being carried out of old Mrs.

94

Given's house and I couldn't understand why she had died 'cos her house hadn't been bombed?'

Rose nodded, 'Yeah, it took me ages to convince you that people also died of old age and illness.'

Tommy smiled, 'I was stupid, wasn't I?'

'No, not really. All you had ever known was war.' She paused and released him from her arms, 'Now come on, you'll be late for your paper round. Your father's already gone off to work.'

★   ★   ★

He had been doing his paper round for just over a year and quite enjoyed it. Arriving at the newsagent's at seven o'clock he picked up his large satchel of papers and set off on his round: mainly the large blocks of flats and houses in Avenue Road. The previous paperboy had a bad accident: he came rushing down the stairs in one block of flats and ran through the glass door while it was shut. He was still in hospital.

Tommy basked in the early morning sunshine, and was soon back home tucking into his porridge, 'What are you getting up to today?' his mother enquired.

'Me and Tiny are going to have a game of

cricket in the street.'

'What all day?'

'Nah!' Tommy laughed, 'We're going over to Lords later to see Middlesex play Somerset. The terrible twins should be batting today.'

Rose was curious 'Who?'

'The Terrible Twins, that's what they call Compton and Edrich!'

Rose Harris nodded her head as though she understood. She knew they went to Lords a lot, but never asked how he afforded it. She thought she already knew the answer, and thought it best not to ask.

Shirley came into the kitchen waving a kaleidoscope, 'Look what I've got.' She boasted, 'Mummy bought it for my birthday!' She put the kaleidoscope to her eye, 'I can see all lovely colours and patterns, it's really pretty.'

Tommy grimaced, 'Oh, I forgot you're seven today, ain't yer!'

Rose shook her heard despairingly at her son, 'You're a fine one. Can't you get her a little something? She is your sister!'

Tommy sulked, 'Maybe, I'll see.' Not knowing what he could get her, even if he had wanted to.

'Come on, madam, I'll drop you off at Auntie Maude's. I've got to get to work.' Rose paused, and waved her finger at her son, 'Make sure you change the flypapers before you go out.'

Tommy pulled a face; he hated taking down the sticky flypapers with all the horrible dead flies on them. He breathed a sigh of relief as the front door closed.

★   ★   ★

Tiny was already waiting when Tommy got to Barrow Hill Road. 'I brought the bat and I found an old tennis ball.'

'Where you bin?' Tiny produced a piece of chalk from his pocket and marked a wicket on the street wall.

'Had to change the fly papers for Mum.'

'Yuk! I hate them things.'

'And then I found a Superman comic what come from America . . .'

Tiny quite understood how that could take any boy's mind off a game of cricket. 'And you forgot all about our game, I suppose.'

'Sorry, pal. How about I let you borrow it?'

'Well . . .'

'I could chuck in a Batman comic, too?'

Tiny couldn't help but be impressed, 'Cor! How did you get hold of 'em?'

'I told you I was writing to a pen friend in America?' His pal nodded. 'Well, I sent them a few Dandy and Beano's and I couldn't believe it when a big parcel of Superman and Batman comics came back in the post. They're much thicker than our measly little things!'

'Wow! Can I borrow all of 'em when you've read 'em?'

Tommy looked very superior, 'Sure.' Handing Tiny the tennis ball, 'Come on, I'll bat and you try and get me out.'

★ ★ ★

An hour or so later, Tiny was at the wicket. 'Right, Tommy, watch this one. I'll really show you how to hit a ball.'

'If I don't bowl you out first!'

True to his word, Tiny knocked the ball into the bombsite opposite, narrowly missing a passing car. It stopped, the driver wound down the window and yelled, 'Who do you think you are? Denis Compton!' Both boys' mouths flew open: it WAS Denis Compton. They rushed over to the car, 'We're going to Lords to see you later, can we have your autograph?' Tiny produced a pencil and a piece of paper, which he tore in half and handed to Tommy, 'Can you put Happy Birthday to Shirley from Denis Compton for my little sister on this one?'

The cricketer looked delighted. 'O.K. lads, and keep practising, you never know one day someone might be asking for your autograph,' and very carefully he signed the two pieces of paper before driving off, leaving two dumbfounded boys.

Tommy stared at his piece of paper, 'I can't believe it! Denis Compton, eh!' Picking up the toy cricket bat he shouted to his pal, who was on the bombsite looking for the tennis ball, 'Throw us the ball and I'll take it indoors so we can go and see a proper match.'

'I think we'll need a bigger bat before we can actually play at Lords. This one gives me a backache.'

'I've had it since I was a little kid.'

'You still are a little kid!'

Tommy laughed, 'All right, lofty. We can't all be beanpoles!'

★ ★ ★

Rose had left a packet of sandwiches on the kitchen sideboard for him. Once outside again the two friends made their way down Barrow Hill Road towards Lords Cricket Ground in Wellington Road. Walking down Cavendish Close at the back of Lords, they climbed over a wall that backed onto one of the houses and ran across the lawn, carefully avoiding the colourful flowerbeds, to another garden wall. Peering over the top, they looked beyond some trees and bushes to another house in which an elderly lady was playing a piano. They crept across that garden, too, and came to the wall that bordered Lords Cricket Ground, climbed it and dropped down into the cricket ground.

Quickly they ran round the ground and strolled nonchalantly by the Tavern, as though they had been there for hours. Tommy pointed excitedly, 'There's empty seats up there in that stand where the posh people go.'

Tiny looked up, 'We've never been in there, have we?'

A wicked gleam appeared in Tommy's eye, 'I bet it's great up there, come on.' They ran through the unguarded entrance, up some stairs and sat down. 'Look, 'the terrible twins' are batting.'

Tommy reached into his pocket and brought out his sandwiches, 'Come on Tiny, tuck in.'

Several spectators muttered and glared at the young enthusiasts, telling them in no uncertain terms to be quiet whilst play was in progress. The Somerset bowler ran up and bowled to Denis Compton who hit the ball to

'Tuck in!'

the boundary; he raised his bat to celebrate his century.

The whole ground gently rippled with polite applause, but much to the annoyance of spectators around them the two boys jumped up and down, shouting and cheering loudly, 'Did you see that! Six!'

'Yeah! What a beauty! He's got a century.'

Completely engrossed in the cricket, they did not notice two distinguished military-looking gentlemen in blazers approach them. The taller one, who had a grey-waxed moustache, glared at them, 'Excuse me, what are you two delinquents doing in our seats?'

His companion was red faced with anger, 'I don't know, you can't even go to the bar for a drink without these hooligans taking your seats. I'll go and fetch the steward, Nigel.'

Tommy quickly blurted out, 'We're sorry, mister, we didn't know anyone was sitting here, honest.' A steward wearing a MCC blazer came hurrying down the steps and grabbed the boys by their collars, 'Come on you two. It's members only in here!' And marched them out of the stand.

Downstairs the steward admonished the boys, 'I bet you two bunked in, didn't you? Where are your tickets?' The two boys, red faced and slightly tearful, looked guiltily at the ground. Then Tommy, snatching at straws, had a thought and mumbled, 'We know Denis Compton.'

The steward laughed, 'Oh yeah! And my uncle's Donald Bradman! Look I should throw you out of the ground, but I'll let you stay until close of play if you help me collect all the seat cushions up afterwards. Then I can go home early, but next time I catch you I'll throw you out of the ground!'

The boys nodded gratefully, 'O.K, mister. And thanks for letting us stay.' The steward beckoned, 'Come on, follow me and I'll show you where you can sit so I can keep an eye on you!'

★　★　★

Sitting on their cushions in the cheap seats the two boys, along with the large crowd, were thoroughly entertained by Compton and Edrich who were in fine form. The boys were so absorbed in the game they were surprised how quickly close of play came. It was soon half past six.

As the spectators slowly left the stand Tiny looked a bit worried, 'I should have been home an hour ago for tea, my mum will go mad!'

Tommy shrugged his shoulders and waved his hand, 'Well, we've got to collect all these cushions from the seats and take them to the steward over there at the store room.'

'It's going to take ages, I'll be in the doghouse!'

'I'm in trouble as well. My mum won't very happy. We don't have tea until my dad comes home from work about six o'clock, but I'll still be late.'

Tiny hurriedly started grabbing cushions off the wooden seats, 'Come on then, let's get on with it!'

★ ★ ★

Nearly an hour later, they were trudging back up St John's Wood High Street, Tiny was looking really worried 'Heaven knows what my parents will say.'

Tommy thought for a moment, 'Well it was worth it, wasn't it? Your Dad likes sport so he's bound to understand when you tell him Compton and Edrich were batting all afternoon. They were brilliant. Hope they play like that against the Aussies.'

His pal brightened up, 'Yeah, but I don't think we can go to Lords tomorrow though, that steward will throw us out!'

Tommy shook his head, 'Never mind, it gets a bit boring if Compton and Edrich aren't batting anyway!'

'I know, but it would be good to see Middlesex win and keep up with Yorkshire.'

'I bet Yorkshire finish top.'

'Bet yer sixpence they don't!'

Tiny thought for a minute, 'O.K,' he agreed as they reached Tommy's flat, 'See yer tomorrow!'

Tommy rang the bell and his mother opened the door, 'You're very late!'

'Sorry, Mum. The ground was packed and it took ages to get out. 'The terrible twins' were batting. Compton got two hundred and fifty two not out and they put on over four hundred, it was brilliant!'

Rose looked unimpressed, 'Come on and have your tea. Everyone else has finished.' Tommy took his coat off, washed his hands and went into the kitchen.

His father was sitting at the table reading a newspaper and Shirley was still looking at her kaleidoscope, 'What did you get me for my birthday?'

Tommy sighed, 'Wait a minute,' and went back to his bedroom. He reappeared clutching a piece of paper, which smiling proudly he enthusiastically gave to his sister, 'Here!'

Shirley looked puzzled and grabbed it, 'Let's see!'

Mother and son waited for Shirley's

reaction, 'Denis Compton? Who's Denis Compton?'

Arthur Harris, who had been studying the racing results, looked up from his newspaper, 'He's the Brylcream boy!' His daughter pulled a face and screwed the autograph up and threw it away in disgust.

Horrified, Tommy turned to his mother and father, 'I get Denis Compton's autograph for her and look what she does! I know kids who would give me a week's pocket money for that!'

Arthur had retrieved the piece of paper and was reading it, 'How did you get this, son? It is real ain't it?' he asked suspiciously.

Tommy explained how they had met their idol. Handing the piece of paper back to his daughter her father reasoned, 'Come on love, keep it, he's really famous. Your brother meant well.'

Shirley took it reluctantly, and stamped her foot. 'I don't want it, I wanted something nice!' and ran out of the kitchen.

Rose glared angrily at her son, 'Look what you've done now, go and talk to her!'

Tommy found his sister sitting in tears on her bed. Thinking quickly how he could retrieve the situation, he sat down next to her, 'Denis Compton is really famous. I bet all your friends will be jealous. I was going to

106

buy you an autograph book tomorrow, and you could collect more autographs of famous people. Lots of kids do it for a hobby. I'll even give you my Bernard Miles one.'

Shirley looked at him suspiciously, 'Will you come and get autographs with me?'

Resignedly, Tommy nodded, 'Of course, Mum won't let you wander around on your own!'

Taking his sister's hand he led her back into the kitchen. 'It's alright, now. I'm going to buy an autograph book for Shirley and we'll stick Bernard Miles's and Denis Compton's in it as her first autographs.' Turning to his postman father Tommy asked, 'Can you tell us some addresses of stars and we can go round to their houses?'

Arthur Harris was concerned, 'Well, I'm not supposed to, but don't tell anyone else and I'll find out a few for you.' His father then asked, 'How much was it to get into Lords?'

His son went red with embarrassment and stuttered, 'We bunked in!'

Arthur laughed, 'Only teasing, I guessed as much, how did you do that?'

A very relieved Tommy boasted, 'We climbed over the walls of the houses in Cavendish Close.'

'Dame Myra Hess lives in one of those houses.'

'Who's she?'

'Don't you know? She's a famous classical pianist and during the war played public concerts in the National Gallery, even when the bombs were falling on London. She was a real morale booster, a musical heroine.'

Tommy's expression changed to one of realisation, 'Oh, we saw some old dear playing a piano, Dad.'

His parents burst into infectious laughter and even Shirley joined in, not quite knowing what she was laughing at, but repeating, 'Some old dear playing a piano, Tommy saw some old dear playing the piano!'

Her brother just smiled, 'I bet she's not as famous as Denis Compton', relieved that the day had ended on a high note.

8

Autograph Hunters

It might have been the sunshine streaming through the bedroom window that awoke Tommy or was it his father getting his bicycle from the shed in the backyard? His mother came into the bedroom with his cup of tea, 'Oh, you're awake are you?' putting the cup on his bedside cabinet. 'You're father's just gone to work.'

'I know I heard him!' Tommy rubbed the sleep from his eyes, 'I didn't have a nightmare last night!'

Mrs. Harris stood by the bedroom door and smiled, 'That's good, ain't it? Sounds like you're over the worse.'

Tommy was soon up, washed and dressed and heading for the front door, 'I'll be back about eight as usual for my breakfast.'

Rose nodded in response, 'We're running out of paper in the lavatory, bring some old newspapers from the shop if you can.'

Tommy made a mental note, shrugged his shoulders and down the road in a flash. With his satchel full of newspapers, he was soon striding down the road in sunshine. One of his deliveries was at Tiny's house where he always knocked and handed the newspaper to his pal's mother. It was no different this morning, 'Morning, Mrs. Evans.'

Tiny's mother did not look her normal cheery self. 'Morning, Tommy.'

'Is he up yet?'

Mrs. Evans shook her head, 'No, he was really late for tea yesterday. He's been warned before about being late, so his father has stopped him from going out today.'

Tommy was disappointed, 'He can't come out at all?'

Tiny's mother shook her head. 'No chance! He might see you tomorrow.'

⋆   ⋆   ⋆

He couldn't go to Lords; if that steward saw him he would be thrown out anyway. So, reluctantly, he started thinking about his promise to Shirley. He dropped off his empty satchel at the newsagent's, bought an autograph book, and picked up some old newspapers to take home.

Back home he gave his mother the bundle of old newspapers, 'Thanks. I'll cut them up later for the lavatory.'

Tommy sat down at the table ready for his

porridge, 'Mum . . . ' he started slowly, 'Did Dad leave a list of addresses of famous people?'

Rose went to the sideboard, 'Yes, it's up here, but there's only two addresses on it at the moment. He'll probably get some more from work today.'

'Tiny's not coming out so I won't be going to Lords. I could take Shirley out with me to try and get autographs.'

His mother looked pleased, 'O.K. I'll let Auntie Maude know on my way to work, she'll be delighted to have a day off. Shirley, come in the kitchen a minute.'

Her daughter came out of her bedroom, rather annoyed, 'What? I was just getting ready.'

'Your brother's looking after you today.'

Shirley was puzzled, 'Why?'

Rose bent down and held her hand, 'You're going to get some autographs like he promised, so you've got to be a good girl.'

Shirley nodded in agreement and looked at her brother, 'Where's my autograph book then?'

Tommy took it out of his pocket, 'There we are, now let me finish my breakfast and we'll be on our way.'

Rose put her coat on, 'I've left some pie in the oven for your lunch. It just needs

111

warming up. Right, I'm off to work now! Behave yourselves!'

Tommy had a look at the list and saw that Googie Withers and John McCallum lived in Avenue Road and the other address was in North Gate. According to his Dad the famous Andrew Sisters were staying there while they were appearing at The London Palladium.

'We'll try Googie Withers's and John McCallum's house first.'

'Who are they?'

Tommy seemed surprised, 'Don't you know? They're film stars, remember when Mum and Dad were talking about that film It Always Rains on Sunday? They were both in it!'

★ ★ ★

As they walked hand in hand along Avenue Road Tommy noticed a smart, expensive car slowly following them. He couldn't understand why, not realising that to a curious stranger they looked like the couple of 'Bisto' kids from the advertising poster. The two little scruffy urchins stood out like sore thumbs in the very select, smart part of St Johns Wood.

It seemed, too, that the area had escaped

A couple of 'Bisto' kids.

the ravages of war with very little bombing; the large expensive houses were still standing. They reached the address on the piece of paper and entered two big iron gates. To their surprise the car followed them in and the driver, wearing dark glasses, pulled up and got out. It was only then that Tommy recognised him as the handsome dark haired film star John McCallum.

His sister had already run ahead and pressed the front door bell, with her autograph book clutched in her other hand. A smiling Googie Withers opened the door as her husband caught up with Tommy and Shirley.

'Can I have your autograph, please?' Shirley pleaded. The film stars laughed and Googie patted her on the head. 'Of course, you're so sweet!' And she signed the book before handing it to her husband.

Tommy looked on in awe. He had seen both Googie Withers's and John McCallum's photos in all the magazines and newspapers. They both made a fuss of his little sister as they handed the book back to her,

'Thanks,' said Shirley wide eyed with excitement. She waved goodbye as the door was shut politely behind the famous couple.

Tommy took his sister's hand, 'Come on.'

Very reluctantly Shirley was led down the

path and out through the big iron gates.

They trudged back home for lunch, 'Where we going this afternoon, Tommy?'

Excitedly he replied, 'We're going to North Gate, to see if the Andrew Sisters are in.'

She was puzzled, 'I don't know them either, but I hope they are as nice as Googie Withers.'

Her brother tried to explain; 'You've heard Freddie playing Boogie Woogie Bugle Boy on the gramophone at home. Well that's them!'

Shirley laughed, 'Mum said that when Freddie was little he took the back off the gramophone to see if there were tiny people inside!'

Her brother smiled and nodded, 'I know, she told me that story, too. The Andrew Sisters have sung with Bing Crosby and have been in films. They've come all the way from America to sing at The London Palladium.'

Shirley was suitably impressed; in her mind America was as far away as the moon.

★ ★ ★

After lunch brother and sister were soon heading for North Gate in Prince Albert Road. Shirley skipped along the pavement practically pulling her brother along with her. At North Gate, they just stood for a while outside the luxurious block of flats on the edge of Regents Park. Feeling very nervous, Tommy led his sister up the carpeted staircase. He pressed the doorbell very gingerly and looked down at Shirley whose eyes were shining with excitement.

The door was opened by one of the Andrew Sisters with a very surprised look on her face. Shirley offered her the autograph book and pen, 'Can I have your autograph, please?' The response was very unexpected as the Andrew Sister called out to her other sisters, 'We've got visitors.' and then ushered Tommy and Shirley inside the palatial flat.

On entering the sitting room Tommy and his sister realised that they had never seen such luxury with decorative mirrors and framed paintings on the walls. They seemed to be walking on air over a floor covered in nice deep carpeting that contrasted greatly with the lino and rugs at home.

'I'm Maxine, this is Patti and Laverne,' said the Andrew Sister who had opened the door. 'Sit down.' she indicated a huge soft sofa that dominated the room. Tommy lifted his sister onto the sofa before practically climbing up himself to sit beside her, sinking back into unknown softness, and realising his feet didn't touch the carpet. Then, to their surprise, Patti came into the room with two glasses of lemonade and some chocolate biscuits.

'How did you know where we were staying?' Laverne enquired. Tommy couldn't believe that the Andrew Sisters appeared to be so interested in them. It was as though the two children were the stars, 'Our Dad's your postman.' Tommy proudly informed Laverne through a mouthful of chocolate biscuit. Meanwhile his little sister was the centre of attention with Patti and Maxine. For about two hours Tommy and Shirley were talking and laughing with the famous Andrew Sisters. Laverne in particular wanted to know all about their lives and especially about how they survived in London during the War.

Tommy was only too happy talking about his wartime experiences, including the time he was evacuated from London. He enjoyed it far more than dreaming about it. The afternoon flew by and when Patti looked at the clock she seemed surprised, 'Gee, is that the time? Sorry, kids, you'll have to go now.' she said reluctantly. The two children took a final swig of lemonade and jumped off the sofa.

All three Andrew Sisters saw them to the front door and then hugged and kissed them both goodbye. Tommy was a bit embarrassed in front of Shirley and thought it was a bit soppy, but knew he would be boasting about it to everyone when he had a chance.

* * *

Brother and sister ran down the stairs into the street and rushed home so excited. When they arrived home Mrs. Harris answered the door, 'Mummy, mummy we've been with the Andrew Sisters!' her daughter shrieked unable to contain her excitement, 'Look! Look!' Shirley continued waving her autograph book at her mother, 'Calm down!' said Mrs. Harris gathering Shirley up in her arms. Tommy was just as excited but was surprised to find he had a lovely contented feeling seeing his sister so happy, 'Come on and tell me all about it!' Mrs. Harris continued as she beckoned them into the sitting room.

The children told their mother all about their exciting afternoon and how nice the Andrew Sisters had been. Mrs. Harris sat engrossed in the story they had to tell. She had been surprised and delighted that Tommy had taken Shirley out for the day as they were always fighting and arguing at home.

That night Tommy went to bed thinking it

hadn't been too bad spending time with his sister. In fact he had quite enjoyed it. He wouldn't tell Tiny that though, he would make out it had been a bit of an ordeal. After all little girls were soppy, even little sisters.

9

Penny For The Guy

It was a cold foggy evening in November and Guy Fawkes night was fast approaching. Tommy and Tiny had finished school for the day and were outside St John's Wood tube station with their home made Guy propped up inside an old pram. 'Penny for the Guy, Mister?'

As people came out of the tube station on their way home from work, the two boys' voices echoed through the cold evening air. Every now and then someone stopped, reached into his pocket and dropped a few coppers into the pram.

The frown on Tommy's face deepened. Concentrating he counted on, 'Five and tuppence, five and thruppence . . . Guess how much we've got so far?'

'Four bob?'

'Five shillings and four pence!'

'Brilliant, let's go and buy some fireworks before the shops shut.'

Tommy thought for a moment, 'But five bob won't buy enough, will it! Is it worth knocking at a few of those prefabs on the way to the shops?

Tiny smiled, 'I don't think so, we never get much there 'cos a lot of 'em are out of work. D'yer remember when they were erected by those German prisoners of war?'

'Yeah! They were put up in one day, just like grown up Meccano sets, weren't they? My dad told me they are made out of material from war damaged aircraft.'

'Are they? Oh, let's give 'em a miss, I don't want to be late for tea. Anyway tonight we are going round the posh flats, ain't we? You know we always get more money there!'

Tommy wheeled the pram back home at great speed, letting it go, and then running with his friend to catch it up shouting, 'Stop the pram! Save our baby sister!'

People passing by were suitably shocked. Several actually stopped it, only to join in the laughter with the two boys when they saw it was only their Guy. Parking the pram outside, they pushed by an elderly customer, impatient to get to the glass display cabinets of pyrotechnics in the sweet shop. 'Watch it, sonny.'

'Sorry, Mister.'

'Kids. I was young meself once.'

'Make sure you get some bangers.' After

Tommy wheeled the pram back home

much deliberation they finally picked out a few Roman Candles, Rockets and Bangers. 'How much are these, Mister?'

'Four and ten, to you, lad.'

They duly handed over their begging proceeds. 'Look at that lot, Tiny. Great ain't they?'

'Now all we need is a bonfire.'

Tiny froze in the shop doorway. 'NO!'

'What up!' Tommy tried to look round his tall but skinny friend.

'The pram!'

'What about it. It's still there ain't it?'

'Yeah, but . . . '

Tommy could not believe his eyes, 'Someone's nicked our Guy!'

Tiny looked gloomily into the empty pram, 'How can we make any money tonight without a Guy?'

'Oh don't worry, I'll think of something!'

'We'll meet at the usual time then?'

Tommy laughed, 'Sure, why not? We can make some more money Guying, somehow!' So saying he put the bag of fireworks in the pram and they made their way home.

★ ★ ★

Later that evening the boys met as arranged, 'Let's go to Charlbert Court and do some Guying.'

123

'How are we going Guying without a Guy, eh? Where's this brilliant idea you were supposed to come up with?'

'I've got an idea all right! You wait and see.' So off they trudged, down the road to Charlbert Court, 'We will just do the top floors!'

Tiny was confused and curious and not to say suspicious, 'Why?'

'I'll walk up to the top floor and ring the doorbells. When someone answers I'll just ask for a penny for the Guy.'

His friend shook his head, 'But we haven't got a Guy.'

'I'll say it's downstairs, but the lifts are not working so I couldn't carry it up the stairs!'

'But the lifts are working!'

Tommy laughed, 'Not if you're down here holding the doors open! It's either that or one of us will have to dress up as a Guy!'

His pal's face lit up, and he dutifully opened the lift doors on the ground floor. Up Tommy went to the top floor and pressed a bell. A cheerful grey haired old man with glasses answered the door to a sad faced little scruffy ten year old, 'Penny for the Guy please, Mister?'

The man looked around, 'Where's the Guy?'

'The lifts aren't working and I couldn't

carry him upstairs, he's too big and heavy.'

The man went over to the lift and pressed the button. Nothing happened, 'Funny, they were working earlier, I'll have to report it in the morning.' Feeling sorry for the lad he reached into his pocket and produced half a crown.

'Thank you, sir, thank you!'

The man smiled and closed his door. One by one, Tommy repeated this at the other flats on the upper floors with similar success. With the coins jangling in his pocket, he ran to find his co-conspirator.

Safely away from the flats, an impatient Tiny asked, 'Did you get anything?'

Tommy put his hand in his pocket and pulled out some silver coins, half crowns and two bob bits, 'Look! There's about a pound there!'

Tiny looked at the money in utter amazement, 'That's more than we get *with* a Guy!'

'I know, but these are posh people. They don't give pennies. Let's try the next block and later we can go to some other posh flats, like Oslo Court.'

Laughing and joking they entered the next block quite confident that they would have equal success.

★ ★ ★

Later that night the boys sat down and checked their ill-gotten gains. 'How much now?'

'Let me see. Five pounds, two shillings and sixpence!' They had never seen such wealth. 'We can buy a lot more fireworks tomorrow.' Tommy remarked as they divided the money between them.

'You've got more than me!'

'I can't help that, just be happy that they gave us silver!'

'Yeah.' Tiny pushed his share inside his pocket, happy in the knowledge that he could not have pulled the scam off the way Tommy had done; 'We'll have a great Guy Fawkes night now!'

'Yeah, we'll have to concentrate on getting stuff for our bonfire over the next few nights. It's not all that big at the moment!'

'We'll talk about it tomorrow at school, who was Guy Fawkes anyway?'

Tommy looked surprised, 'Don't yer know? My mum said he tried to blow up Parliament years ago and it's a pity he didn't.'

'At least it's a good job he tried or we wouldn't have all this fun on fireworks night would we?' Tiny laughed, and kicked a stone down the road, 'I wonder what the time is?'

In all the excitement Tommy had forgotten about time, 'We'd better go home now, we must have been out quite a while. My Mum goes potty if I'm out after eight!'

His pal smiled, 'Come on, I'll race you to the top of the street!'

* * *

The two boys spent the next couple of evenings collecting wood and cardboard from wherever they could for the bonfire they, and other children, were building on a deserted bombsite.

* * *

'Tonight's the night, Tiny! November the fifth at last!'

'Yeah. It won't be long now before it gets dark and we can light the bonfire.'

'Some of the kids in our street have promised to run round the shops for some more wood and stuff.'

'Come on, let's get all these cardboard boxes broken up.'

With a much engineering precision as any young lad is capable, Tommy threw another pile of rubbish on the heap. 'What's that!'

'What's what?'

'I thought I heard a cry.'

'What sort of cry?'

'If you'd only shut up for a minute I might

be able to find out.'

'Yeah. I can hear it now. It's coming from the inside of the bonfire.'

'I definitely heard a meow that time.' Getting down on his hands and knees Tommy crawled inside, and found a frightened tabby kitten. 'Gently does it. Don't worry I'm not going to hurt you. There, there.' He gently tickled the little creature behind its ears and cuddled it to his chest.

'Ain't he cute. He must have got lost or something!'

'Finders keepers! I'll take him home and see if my Mum will let me keep him!' With the kitten safely tucked inside his zip up jacket he shoved his cold hands in his trouser pockets, 'Right, I'll see you here after tea with our fireworks. My Mum helped me to make a new Guy that we can put on top of the bonfire.'

'Bonfire night's great, ain't it! We can stay out late and everything!'

Tommy smiled at the kitten, and stroked the fluffy head poking out of his jacket. Silently he hoped and prayed, 'Make my Mum let me keep my kitten.'

★ ★ ★

He arrived rang the bell with fingers crossed.

'Oh, it's you.' Then seeing the little kitten's

head poking out from her son's jacket, Rose asked suspiciously. 'Where did you get that?'

'It's all right mum, I found it in the bonfire, honest!' And putting on the puppy dog face he knew his mother found hard to resist, he pleaded, 'Can I keep it? Please Mum, I could call it Guy after Guy Fawkes!'

Shirley came running out of the sitting room, 'Ah ain't it lovely! Let me stroke it.'

Their mother looked at both of them and relented, 'O.K, but I don't know what your father will say!'

The children were overjoyed, 'Thanks, Mum.'

Rose wagged a finger at them, 'But if we find out who it belongs to you'll have to give it back!'

Her son looked rather disappointed, 'All right, I'm gonna make him a little bed in a cardboard box,' and disappeared into his bedroom.

During tea Shirley begged her mother, 'Why can't I go out tonight and see the fireworks?'

Rose shook her head, 'I've told you, you are too young! We'll watch them in the sky from the front steps and you can let off some sparklers!' And a disappointed Shirley had to watch her brother collect his fireworks together.

Sadly he said goodbye to Guy the kitten. 'I'm going now, Mum.'

'O.K make sure you're back by ten o'clock and be careful.'

Putting his fireworks in the pram with his homemade Guy he left the flat, and called to his mother in the kitchen, 'Yes, Mum.'

She shook her head and smiled, 'As though butter wouldn't melt in his mouth.'

★   ★   ★

A crowd of children gathered round to look at Tommy's Guy, 'Come on then, let's put it on top of the bonfire and then we can set light to it.'

The boys pulled the Guy out of the pram and scrambled over wood and cardboard to, finally, put it on the top of the bonfire. To loud cheers from children adults alike, the two friends quickly scrambled down. And with excited anticipation Tiny handed Tommy a box of matches and they steadily made their way around the bonfire in opposite directions, lighting any odd bits of newspaper that protruded at knee height or below.

As if this was the signal everyone had been waiting for, they started lighting fireworks all over the bombsite. Rockets flared towards the stars from countless milk bottles. And

Catherine Wheels that had previously been nailed to various posts twirled around at great velocity showering countless vivid colours into frenzied spinning patterns.

'Cor, ain't they smashing.'

'What about ours?'

'This girl's Dad has a lot to light. Let's watch hers first and have ours later.'

Before long Tommy and Tiny were impatient to join in the fun. 'It's not the same as lightin' them yerself, is it?'

'Nah! Look over there. Give us some matches.' Quietly they crept up behind the unsuspecting young girls, dropped a lit banger or two and quickly retreated to a safe distance.

They shrieked with laughter, 'I don't know what was louder, their screams or the bangers.'

'It's great fun, ain't it,' Tommy said to his friend who couldn't agree more.

'Yeah, some of those soppy girls only light little sparklers. They're not real fireworks, are they?'

'No! Not like ours!'

★ ★ ★

The bonfire was really burning now and had collapsed in places. Tiny noticed flames had

131

nearly reached the Guy, 'Come on, let's watch the Guy burn.'

Enthusiastically they both joined the crowd nearer the bonfire. They must have been standing at least ten yards away, but the heat from the blaze was so intense it cut through the cold night air and scorched their faces, giving their cheeks a cherry glow.

Through the sound of fireworks and the crackle of the fire they heard a woman calling, 'Timmy! Timmy! Puss! Puss!' And when they turned around there was a little old lady wearing an old overcoat and mittens, crying and shrieking helplessly to people, 'I can't find my kitten. Oh, what if he hid in the fire! Oh my poor Timmy!'

The boys looked at each other helplessly. 'Are you thinking what I'm thinking?' Tommy asked.

His friend nodded, 'You'll have to tell her mate, you can't keep it!'

Tommy had already come to that conclusion, and he went over to the little old lady, 'He's alright, miss.'

The old lady was too distraught to take in what he was saying, 'No, the last few days when I've let him out I've found him hiding in the bonfire! Now he's disappeared altogether.' Bursting into tears again, 'He must be in there! My poor little kitten is dead!'

Tommy, feeling very guilty, valiantly tried to console the old lady, 'Really, it's alright miss. I found him earlier and took him home.'

The old lady stopped crying and looked at him in disbelief, 'You mean . . . '

Tommy interrupted her, 'Yes, he's safe! Come with me and I'll take you to him!' Taking her hand they slowly walked off the bombsite towards his home.

Mrs Harris opened the door, 'You're home early . . . ' Her voice trailed off as she saw the little old lady with her son.

Tommy blurted out in one breath, 'Mum, Guy belongs to this lady, except his name is Timmy and she thought he had been burned in our bonfire.'

Rose held her hand up, 'Hold on, I'll go and get the kitten and you can tell me all about it.'

In the sitting room Arthur Harris was engrossed in his newspaper. 'Hello, what's all this?' he enquired. After suitable explanations, Arthur got up and gestured to his empty chair, 'Sit down, Miss . . . um.'

The elderly woman smiled for the first time, 'It's Mrs. Parry, but I lost my husband in the war!'

Arthur felt her sadness, 'Let me have your coat and I'll get you a cup of tea.'

Rose came into the room carrying the tabby kitten.

Mrs, Parry jumped to her feet and burst into tears, of happiness this time; she took the kitten and clasped it to her chest, 'Oh thank you, thank you so much!' And turning to Tommy she kissed him on the cheek, 'You're such a little hero!'

Rose Harris smiled, 'Yes, I'm really proud of him!'

Tommy who had been feeling so sad at losing his new found pet suddenly felt ten feet tall. His father came into the room carrying a tray with three cups of tea, 'Is it your kitten?' he enquired of Mrs. Parry.

'Oh it certainly is! Thanks to your little boy he's alive and well!'

Mr. Harris laughed, 'It's about time he done something right for a change!'

'But don't you see? If your son hadn't pulled Timmy out of the bonfire, he probably would have been burned alive.'

Tommy pulled a face, 'Mum's proud of me!' and swaggered to the door, 'I'm going back to the bonfire now, is that alright, Mum!'

'Of course it is, take no notice of your Dad, he's pleased really! We'll see you later.'

Mrs. Parry beamed across at her little hero, 'I'm staying for a little while so your Mum and Dad can tell me all about you.'

Tommy left the flat with a broad smile on his face just eager to get back to his friend and enjoy being a hero on bonfire night.

10

Election Fever

January 1949 started very badly, as far as Tommy's parents were concerned, when Tommy Handley unexpectedly died. Rose was a huge fan of the comedian and Tommy was surprised at the grief shown by his Mum, and the cloud of sadness that hung around their home for quite some time afterwards. His Mum's reaction to the news made him think that he had been named after Tommy Handley, but he never asked his parents if this were true.

The good thing about 1949 was that his brother Freddie was demobbed from the Army. He should have been demobbed earlier, but because of trouble in Palestine, or something Tommy didn't understand, he had to serve another six months. It meant sharing a bedroom again, but it was worth it: he was enthralled with all the stories about life in the Army that his brother had to tell.

Freddie also made him a bike, which he called an A.S.P.: 'all spare parts'. It was made up of the good parts from various bikes dumped on building sites and waste ground.

The worst of the winter was over, and he was riding home from his morning paper round on this lovely April day. Freddie, who had been in the Royal Signals, had already left for work with an electrical company when Tommy arrived home.

At breakfast Rose reminded her son about his eleven plus exam that he had taken a few weeks ago, 'When will you get your results?'

He shrugged his shoulders, 'Don't know, any day now I guess!' Tommy wasn't really interested. As long as he went to the same school as Tiny he was not worried.

Rose Harris had a lot on her mind at the moment. It was not only her son's education that occupied her thoughts, she was standing in the local council elections as a Labour candidate.

Shirley and Tommy finished their breakfast, picked up their dinner money and left home with a hurried goodbye. 'Are we going to help Mummy with the election tonight?' Shirley asked excitedly.

'Yeah, I'll get Tiny to help as well.'

During the last year, brother and sister seemed to be getting along much better. Parting company inside their school they went to their separate classes. As usual it was very rowdy and noisy; Tommy entered his classroom and sat down at his desk next to his friend.

'Alright, Tommy?'

'Yeah, what you doing tonight?'

'Nothing much!'

'Me and my sister are helping Mum with her election stuff, d'yer fancy coming?'

Tiny thought for a moment, 'Does Shirley have to come with us? You know what she's like sometimes!'

Tommy smiled and said with a dismissive air, 'She's not too bad now, yer know!'

'O.K I might as well.'

'Come on, cheer up, it'll be a bit of a laugh.'

Mr. Phipps, their English teacher, walked in and silence fell over the whole classroom; desks were closed and everyone sat to attention. 'Right, everyone, get your textbooks out,' Mr Phipps barked. Tommy was ready for another boring day, and eagerly looked forward to the going home bell.

Finally the magic hour of four o'clock had arrived and the last lesson was just ending. The classroom was buzzing with chitchat. Miss Beck, the music teacher, had a pile of envelopes in front of her. She banged on her desk shouting, 'Quiet, you lot, quiet!'

Miss Beck didn't seem to command the same respect as Mr. Phipps, but then she had never thrown her wooden backed board-duster at anybody.

Trying to look as stern as possible Miss Beck picked up the envelopes on her desk, 'These contain the results of your eleven plus exam. Form a queue and I will hand them out to you as you leave the classroom. *You* mustn't open them. Give them to your parents to open, O.K?' So saying she stood by the classroom door and gave one to each of the apprehensive children.

The two boys were walking through the playground clutching their results when Tommy saw his sister having an argument with an older, rough-looking boy. He was pushing her around.

Shirley might be a soppy little girl, but she was also Tommy's sister. He felt a sudden rush of anger. 'What yer doing?' He shoved the boy away from her.

Shirley chimed in, 'We were playing marbles and he pinched some of mine and won't give them back to me.'

He might have been older than Tommy, but the other boy looked scared of the angry brother. 'I won 'em, honest,' he said very limply.

'Nah yer didn't.' Shirley screamed.

Tommy grabbed the boy's hand and forced some marbles from it, and gave them to

Shirley who put them in her marble-bag. Tommy poked his finger at the boy, 'Don't yer ever touch my sister again! D'yer hear?'

Shirley looked at her brother in amazement; he had never been so supportive before. The boy scowled and wandered off, muttering something under his breath. Tommy waved his envelope, 'Come on, Sis, let's go home; I've got my exam results here. I'll see you tonight, Tiny, about seven.'

★   ★   ★

Excited, Tommy shouted through the letter-box, 'Mum! We're home, I've got my results.'

Rose hurriedly opened the front door. They all rushed into the sitting room where she opened the vital envelope, and unfolded the enclosed sheet of paper printed in green ink. Slowly she read . . . Gradually an enormous smile filled her face, 'You've passed. You can go to a Grammar School or even a Polytechnic. I've heard Regent Street Polytechnic is very good. It'll be brilliant if you can go there. I just can't believe it!'

Tommy was just happy that his Mum was pleased, but frowned as he thought, 'I wonder if Tiny passed.'

That evening, Arthur Harris came home from work to an excitable wife, 'Tommy's passed his eleven plus.' She showed her husband the contents of the envelope, 'Look, he can even go to the Polytechnic in Regent's St. if he likes!'

Arthur peered through his glasses, but took the news very calmly. 'Why are you surprised? He must have his father's brains,' he said jokingly.

'Some hopes,' his wife replied glibly.

*　*　*

The evening meal still warm in their stomachs, Tommy and Shirley asked, 'What do you want us to do, Mum?'

'Yes, Mum'll be famous when she wins the election and becomes a councillor.'

'Go to the Labour Party Committee Rooms and they will give you some leaflets. Make sure you deliver them to the addresses printed on them.'

Tommy thought for a moment, 'Do the Tories have leaflets as well?' he enquired, 'Of course they do!' his mother replied with a puzzled look on her face.

The children headed for the front door, with their mother shouting after them, 'I'll see you at the Committee Rooms later on.'

Tiny was waiting at the corner, looking very unhappy. Tommy called out to him, 'Hi yer, did yer pass the exam?'

His pal shook his head, 'No, I've got a list of secondary schools.'

Tommy's face fell; he wished he had failed, too. 'Blast! I passed and my Mum wants me to go to Regent Street Polytechnic in the West End. Hope it ain't too posh,' he said gloomily.

Tiny was envious, 'You lucky thing, my parents are really upset.'

Tommy was adamant, 'I wish I had failed, I wanted to go to the same school as you!'

Shirley, who was standing there silently, suddenly piped up, 'Come on, lets go and get these leaflets!'

Later that evening all three of them delivered leaflets around St Johns Wood and returned to the Labour Party Committee Rooms. Tommy and Shirley found it strange seeing their mother's picture on posters around the room, especially alongside a large photograph of Clement Atlee the Prime Minister, but they couldn't see their mother anywhere. Tommy approached Lady Lucan, 'Where's my Mum?'

Lady Lucan looked surprised, 'Don't you know? Your Mum is out canvassing on a soapbox at the corner of Charlbert St., trying to get more support.'

Outside, in the street, Tommy was puzzled, 'It's funny, ain't it. Lady Lucan's quite ordinary. No different to our Mum really?'

Shirley thought about it, 'Yeah, she's not hoity-toity, and doesn't wear a tiara or anything, like they do in my comics.'

Tommy laughed, 'Come on let's go and see Mum.'

They could just see their mother's head above a crowd of people and heard her shouting, 'And what about the people still living in prefabs. They were supposed to be temporary places for the homeless. Ain't it about time they had new council houses to live in!' Some of the crowd started cheering, drowning out the few voices of dissent. Tommy and Shirley were waving their arms at their mother, but Rose Harris was so zealously engrossed in her speech she didn't notice her children's efforts to attract her attention.

Tiny, who had been very quiet, spoke, 'I've just remembered, I've got to go to the Tory Party Committee Rooms and ask them to send a car to take my parents to the polling booth.'

Tommy and Shirley looked curious, 'They don't vote Tory do they?'

His friend grinned, 'No! Of course not! But they always take up the offer of a lift, and then vote Labour!' Tommy and Shirley shrieked with delight.

A few minutes later all three were outside the Conservative Committee Rooms. Tiny went inside, where a large intimidating picture of Winston Churchill looked down at him, and spoke to a very smart lady. After she had written down the address and the time his parents wanted the car to call he came out to his two friends. 'Good job I remembered that!'

Tommy turned to his sister, 'I had an idea this morning when Mum mentioned the leaflets, come on!' And they both went into the Committee Rooms leaving a dumbstruck Tiny outside.

'Have you any leaflets we can deliver?'

The lady eyed him suspiciously, and then a look of recognition came into her eyes, 'You're Mrs. Harris's children aren't you? Why would you want to deliver our leaflets?'

Tommy panicked, grabbed his sister's hand and pulled her out the door.

All three children ran down the street and hid behind some dustbins.

'What was that all about?'

'I thought it might help Mum if they gave us a lot of the leaflets addressed to flats and we threw them in the dustbins. Then they might not vote Tory.'

'You don't think Mum will get elected then, even with Lady Lucan helping her?'

'Vote, Vote, Vote and Vote for Labour,
    Kick the Tories out the door.'

Shirley gloomily asked her brother.

'Nah, Mum said the Tories always win in St Johns Wood.'

Tiny didn't understand, 'Why is she standing for Labour then?'

Tommy shrugged his shoulders, ''Cos she has always belonged to the Labour Party. She reckons they stand up for the working class, but Lady Lucan ain't working class, is she? I don't really understand politics and all that stuff. Labour won the General Election, but in St John's Wood they're always the underdogs!'

Tiny pondered deeply, 'Yeah, she's just like my Dad.'

'What d'yer mean?'

His pal spluttered and tried to explain himself, 'Well, if a little team plays a big team in the F.A Cup he always wants the little team to win!'

Tommy couldn't quite understand the reasoning, 'Come on if Mum's the underdog, let's give her a helping hand.' He picked up a couple of dustbin lids and started banging them together singing, 'Vote, Vote, Vote and Vote for Labour, Kick the Tories out the door.'

Shirley and Tiny joined in as they marched in single file through the streets of St Johns Wood much to the amusement of the voters making their way to the polling station.

11

A Long Weekend

'We want the King!'

Tommy, his parents, brother and sister were squeezed even tighter together. Thousands and thousands of people had thronged outside Buckingham Palace.

A sea of faces laughed and chanted, 'We want the King!'

'We want the King!' Everyone was waving flags and banners. A ripple of bangs bombarded their ears, but no one sought cover.

'Oooh! Aaah!' Instead of fear, joy and laughter exploded spontaneously.

Tommy removed his hands from his head, opened his eyes and looked up into the most wonderful sight he had ever seen. A riot of brilliant lights in colours of every hue lit up the night sky. Each new whoosh and crump gave birth to a fresh burst of florescence, vying for space in the spectators' attention. His jaw dropped in amazement and when he was able to find his voice he joined in the song and sobbed,

'We want the King!'

A pregnant silence was followed by a grand crescendo of cheers and he knew . . . he knew that the King and Queen had come out onto the balcony.

It was the end of the War. Tommy had never seen such happiness, some unashamedly crying. He found himself being lifted up into his father's strong arms. 'There, lad. Can you see now?' No longer able to hide their emotions, father and son hugged each other, their faces wet with mingled tears of joy.

A lone voice heralded, 'Princesses Margaret and Elizabeth are outside the gates!'

Again the crowd cheered.

Everyone surged forward, frantic to catch a glimpse of the young princesses. Tommy and his sister were lifted above the crowd. Peering over hundreds of heads and flat caps through a sea of red, white and blue, he thought he could see them. Excitedly he pointed, 'Look. Mum . . .'

'Another dream?'

Tommy laughed, 'Yeah, but it was a good dream this time. It was VE Day and it was great!'

'That would have been May 1945. Four years ago . . . Rose's own thoughts took her back to that never to be forgotten day. 'Come on, don't forget you are going away today!'

Her young son immediately jumped out of bed and headed for the bathroom.

'You haven't packed your suitcase yet!'

As a reward for passing his eleven plus his parents had paid for a weekend camping holiday in Ongar, Essex, organised by the Co-op. Not only that, but his best friend Tiny had also managed to persuade his parents to let him go, too. Tommy's joy knew no bounds; he had not been away without his parents since he was evacuated.

'You ready yet?' he heard his mother call from the sitting room.

He rammed the last bit of clothing in his case and locked it, 'Coming Mum!'

Tommy and Rose met up with Tiny and his mother, and travelled to Bethnal Green by tube to catch the coach. Impatient to climb aboard the boys suffered their over protective mothers' hugs and kisses. 'Look after yourselves and don't get into any mischief.'

Waving goodbye through the coach window they did little to reassure their anxious parents, 'Don't worry. We'll be OK. You know us!' Their mothers slowly disappeared into the distance.

A stern older man with glasses stood at the front of the coach with a pretty dark haired woman. 'My name's Mrs. Jacks, but you can call me Betty. And this is Mr. Dixon, but he'll be Ken to you. We will be looking after you for the next three days.' She paused for breath, 'Now, I'm coming round to collect your tickets, so I can check them against my list.'

'It's gonna be great, ain't it?' Tiny said.

'Yeah, we'll be like Red Indians in the cowboy films sleeping in a tent. At night we'll probably hear the cries of wild animals, hope it's not too scary.'

The noise level rose and they noticed there were quite a few giggling girls on the coach. Tiny pulled a face, 'Ugh! Why have they let soppy girls on this holiday?'

But Tommy was surprised that he felt quite pleased as he found himself staring at a couple of girls with long blonde hair, 'Come on Tiny, they might be a laugh!'

'Who yer looking at mate?' one girl yelled very aggressively.

Tommy turned beetroot. A girl, especially a nice looking girl, had never spoken to him like that before. But then he had never thought of any girl as pretty before. Red faced he shyly stuttered, 'Nothing, I just wondered what you were laughing at.'

The girls looked at each other and giggled again, 'We were just laughing at how tall your mate is, he's taller than our dad! What's his name?'

Tommy relaxed with a smile, 'Tiny!'

The girls roared with laughter.

'That's only his nickname!'

One of the girls wiped her eyes, 'What's his real name?'

Anxiously Tiny put his hand over his pal's mouth, 'Don't tell her!'

Tommy pushed his hand away, 'He only likes being called Tiny!'

'O.K, but I bet it's something stupid!'

Tommy felt unusually comfortable in their presence; 'We'll tell you at the end of the holiday, maybe!'

Tiny seemed eager to change the subject, 'What's your names then, girls?'

They exchanged glances, 'I'm Debbie and this is my older sister Maggie,' answered the prettier of the two.

Her sister angrily pulled a face, 'Margaret! My name's Margaret and I'm only a year older than you!'

'I'm Tommy by the way! Tiny's my mate and we both live in the Wood.' Debbie looked curious, 'The Wood? What wood?'

'Oh sorry! St John's Wood!'

'Oh so you're the boys from The Wood, very posh. We live in common as muck Mile End.'

Apologetic Tiny butted in aggressively, 'We're not posh, we only live in council flats!'

Tommy felt a strange urge to impress Debbie and continued talking: telling her how he had passed his exams and his mother had decided he was going to Regent Street Polytechnic after the school holidays. Tiny and Margaret were also in deep conversation as the coach continued its uninterrupted journey.

★ ★ ★

The camping site occupied a large field, surrounded by leafy woods on one side and a country road on the other. The two boys, with their newfound friends, left the coach and were impressed to see an array of tents organised in nice long rows and one large marquee dividing them into two sections.

'Children, children,' Betty shouted, 'collect your suitcases from the driver and go to the marquee.' They all joined a mad scramble at the back of the coach.

'Where're the girls?'

'Dunno. I didn't see 'em go.'

'Hurry up, you boys, you're keeping everyone waiting.'

'OK, Miss.' Tiny picked up his case and looked around again.

'They'll probably have gone to the marquee.'

'Yeah, we'd better get a move on.'

* * *

Betty and Ken were on a small platform trying to make themselves heard over the noisy children, 'Quiet! Quiet!' his voice boomed out. The boys clutched their suitcases and awaited instructions; 'You've been allocated one tent to two children. Boy's are to the left of the marquee and the girls on the right. Anyone caught in the wrong section will be sent home.'

Betty took over, waving a clipboard at her young audience, 'All the tents are numbered and if you come up here when your name's called I'll give you a slip of paper with your tent number on it. All meals will be in this marquee supplied by the outside caterers from Ongar. There are portable buildings right at the back of the camping area with separate lavatories and washing facilities for boys and girls!'

Ken looked sternly over his glasses, 'Now, I want no trouble on this holiday. I'll be in the large tent on the boy's side and Betty will be in the large tent on the girl's side. If you have any problems, don't hesitate to come and talk to us. Is that clear?'

The young woman looked quizzically at the children, 'Any questions?'

Everyone looked at each other in complete silence.

'Right, lunch will be served here in two hours. Now when you hear your name, come and collect your tent number.' Betty continued reading a long list of names, 'Tommy Harris and Rupert . . . ' his surname was drowned out by the roar of children's laughter.

Tiny, by far the tallest child in the marquee, stood out like a shining red beacon amongst a sea of pale faces. Inwardly he cursed his parents. Tommy felt so sorry for his friend. As they walked up to collect their tent details he glanced into the crowd and caught sight of the girls. Both laughed and looked away.

Once inside their tent Tommy tried to console his friend and put an arm around him, 'Don't worry, they will soon forget about it.'

'Of course they won't, I'll be the laughing stock of the camp. I'll get all the Rupert the Bear jokes I used to get when I first went to school!'

'Come on let's put our things away!'

Tiny opened his suitcase, 'I wish I was going home!'

Tommy playfully pushed him onto his camp bed, 'Cheer up, I'm here aren't I? We're mates, aren't we? We've been through worst things than a bit of name calling!'

The lorn lad nodded half-heartedly; trying to lift his spirits he smiled weakly and he looked around the tent, 'This is brilliant, ain't it?'

Tommy nodded in agreement, 'Hope it's warm enough at night though!'

* * *

'Let's go and meet some of the other kids.'

Some boys were hanging around the washrooms, as soon as they saw Tiny they yelled out, 'Where's your scarf and check trousers Rupert?'

The victim glowered and looked at Tommy for support, 'Ignore them. They'll soon get fed up.'

'Look over there!
If you dare!
Can you see Rupert Bear?'

Without warning Tiny turned round and rushed at the boys with his fists flying. Pandemonium broke out as Tommy rushed to help him and the fighting soon spilled out into the open field. The two boys, outnumbered by three to one, were putting up a good fight, but still getting the worst of it. Some of the girls had left their washroom and were shouting and cheering them on until a familiar booming voice rang out, 'You lads! Stop it!' And Ken pulled the boys apart.

All the other boys ran off. Ken's angry face loomed in front of them, 'What's this all about?'

'It's his name, sir. He can't help it.'

'It's always been the same. I hate my parents sometimes.'

'Now, now. That's not necessary. I expect you were named after someone else in the family. A grandparent, for instance.'

'Dunno, sir.'

'Anyway, I will not tolerate bullying.' Ken sympathised, 'I had to put up with enough of it myself at school. I'll have a word with everyone at lunch.' He patted them on the head, 'Now go and clean yourselves up!'

It was only then the boys realised they had quite a few cuts and bruises around their faces. They were wiping the blood away with their handkerchiefs when the two girls came over and looked at them admiringly. 'Cor, you can't 'arf fight!' Debbie remarked adoringly as her sister took out her hankie and wiped Tiny's lip.

Immediately Tommy felt a lot better. Perhaps Tiny's problems had been a blessing in disguise. And through his bruised and cut lips he managed, 'We're just going to clean up and then we'll see you at lunch, O.K, girls.'

The girls thought about it ... 'Okey dokey.'

Tiny looked at his pal with a huge grin and whispered thankfully, 'They didn't call me Rupert!'

Tommy playfully punched his friend, 'I told you so, everything's going to be fine!'

★   ★   ★

'I'm starving!'

'It's country air what does it. I wonder what we'll get.'

Walking into the marquee for lunch they spotted Debbie waving to them 'Here, we've saved some seats!'

A few of the boys glowered at them, but there were no mickey-taking.

Mr. Dixon stood on the platform and raised his hand; 'Quiet please!' A hush fell over the children. 'There was a nasty incident this morning at the washrooms.' He stared intently at his audience, 'I want you all to be friends. Any more fighting, or other bad behaviour, and those individuals responsible will be sent home. And, I can assure you, your parents will not be very pleased about paying for a wasted holiday!'

Betty then mounted the platform and took over, 'After lunch your time is your own to have a look around the countryside or just to get to know each other!' As she was talking the caterers took round plates of corn beef and salad, and bowls of bread.

It was not until they started eating that they realised how hungry they were and soon their plates were empty. 'It's a pity there weren't any chips like we get at home,' Debbie remarked.

Her sister was staring intently at the boys, 'Have you got girl friends at home?'

Tommy grimaced, 'Nah, we think girls are soppy.' Then enthusiastically he looked directly at Tiny, 'Fancy investigating the woods this afternoon?'

Before his pal could answer the girls scoffed, 'Yeah, sure!'

The boys looked at each other blankly and then burst out laughing, 'Oh all right then! I guess we'll have to put up with you!' Tommy tried not to show it, but for some reason he couldn't explain, he was happy the girls were coming along.

After lunch they all made their way across the field towards the woods. It was a lovely summer's day. Suddenly a rabbit ran out of the grass in front of them; the girls screamed with surprise.

'It's only a rabbit!'

They laughed and ran after it as it bounded away.

'Don't be silly, you won't catch it.'

Exhausted they all paused for breath at the edge of the woods.

Tiny was the first to speak; 'I wonder what other animals are in the woods.'

Putting his hands up in front of him like claws, Tommy jumped up and roared like a bear. The girls giggled, 'You're mad, there's no bears in Essex!'

Tiny ventured further in amongst the trees, 'Come on, let's see if we can see any squirrels or anything!'

'Let's play hide and seek!'

The girls looked worried, but before they could object, it was decided. 'Yeah, count to twenty and then come and look for us.'

And with that the boys ran through the undergrowth to a clearing where they were soon climbed up amongst the lower branches of a tall tree and waited in silence. The two girls came through the bushes searching for them with worried looks on their faces, 'Tommy where are you?'

'We give up, where are you?' The two boys jumped down from the branches, in front of them; the girls screamed.

Two gypsy lads came running through the trees, 'What's going on?' And seeing Debbie and Margaret he asked, 'Are you girls O.K?'

'Yeah, we're only playing about!'

The gypsy lads looked relieved, 'Thank God for that, we heard such a scream we thought someone was in trouble.'

Tommy smiled, 'No, we're all friends. I'm Tommy and this is Tiny,' then pointing to the girls, 'Debbie and Margaret,'

'I'm Jake and he's my brother Seth.'

The two girls giggled shyly, 'We're sisters.'

'We don't meet many people in these woods, where are you from?' The gypsy boys listened intently at the explanation for the invasion of Londoners.

Margaret was fascinated by the gypsies: with their long curly hair, rings in their ears and large colourful neckerchiefs, they should have looked scruffy, but it suited them. A couple of years older than any of the boys from London, they had a self-assurance lacking in the young campers.

Tiny, for some reason he couldn't explain, felt annoyed at Margaret's interest, broke the silence, 'Where are you from, Seth?'

'We're from everywhere. At the moment our caravans are a couple of miles away.

We've been there a few months; we're probably moving on soon!'

Sitting around on a couple of fallen tree trunks the youngsters nattered about their differing life styles. Seth pulled out a packet of Weights, 'Anyone want a fag?'

'No thanks!'

He put two cigarettes in his mouth, lit them, and passed one to his brother. Jake looked at the two boys, 'Come on, have a fag! Don't be cissies! You're on holiday!'

The girls chimed in, 'Yeah, let's be devils!' and the four took cigarettes from the gypsy lad.

Seth passed his matches to Tommy who thought he'd show Debbie that he could outdo the gypsy, 'Let's have your fags then.'

Obediently, Tiny and the girls passed him their cigarettes. Tommy put all four in his mouth, struck a match, lit them and sucked in like the gypsy boy had done. Instantly, he choked on such a volume of smoke, spitting out the cigarettes. He held his neck, and his face went redder and redder as he coughed. The more he coughed the more the gypsy lads laughed. Debbie rushed to his side, 'Tommy, Tommy you all right?'

Trying to hide his humiliation, 'It's all right, I'm O.K!'

Jake was still grinning, 'You should give up

161

smoking til you grow up.'

Debbie stared at him scornfully, 'I don't fink that's funny!'

Seth butted in, 'It wasn't our fault, he was just trying to show off! Look it's Saturday today. Meet us here tomorrow about two o'clock and we'll make up for it.'

The boys looked at him suspiciously, 'How?'

Seth touched his nose knowingly, 'We'll take you to some old quarry we found and have some fun.'

Walking back to the campsite Tommy was concerned, 'What d'yer think? Reckon we should turn up tomorrow?'

Tiny shrugged his shoulders, 'I don't really trust them, d'you?'

The girls did not agree. 'They're O.K, just a bit wild!'

'Yeah, I think they're lovely. They're different . . . exciting!'

Debbie, her eyes shining, agreed, 'I know they're gypsies, but they mean well. After all they did come to help us when they heard us screaming.'

Tommy shook his head grimly, 'O.K we'll go, but we don't really know them so we'll have to be careful!'

★ ★ ★

'See yer at tea.'

'We'll save your seats!'

Back in their tent Tommy asked, 'What do you think of the girls?'

'I dunno! I've never been this friendly with girls before!' Tiny thought about it for a while. 'But I quite like Margaret, she seems different to the girls at school!'

Tommy smiled, 'Yeah, I feel the same about Debbie. I don't know why, it's a funny feeling, ain't it?'

After tea the children collected wood and gathered round a large bonfire. Betty passed around song sheets and led the singing while Ken accompanied her on a guitar; and in the tradition of such camps, 'Maybe it's because I'm a Londoner', 'Underneath the Arches', 'It's a long way to Tipperary' and 'She's coming round the mountain', rang out. With their arms round each other, the four friends joined in, and thoroughly enjoyed themselves.

With his hands cupped round a mug of hot chocolate, Tommy yawned and declared, 'I enjoyed that, but I'm out of breath and tired now.'

'Yeah, so are we!' the other three all agreed.

Tommy called good night to the girls, 'See you at breakfast.'

'Goodnight!' Then without warning Debbie kissed Tommy very lightly on the cheek.

Margaret followed her lead and brushed Tiny's cheek softly with her lips. Both girls then laughed and ran away to their tent. In the darkness the embarrassed boys could feel their faces glowing like the embers of the dying fire.

'You boys, off to bed now!' Ken shouted as he doused the remains of the fire with a bucket of water.

★   ★   ★

Once in bed Tommy broke the silence, 'I've never been kissed by a girl before.'

'No, neither have I,' and Tiny added thoughtfully, 'I've always thought it silly!'

Tommy smiled, 'It feels nice though, don't it?'

His friend nodded solemnly, and they both closed their eyes and drifted off into a land of sweet dreams and a deep sleep.

Waking up in the early hours of the morning Tommy was desperate to go to the lavatory. Quickly pulling on a pair of trousers he left the tent, as he passed Ken's tent he heard faint voices. One was a female voice and, although he couldn't hear what was being said, he was sure he recognised it. Yawning he quickly ran to the lavatory, but on returning to his own tent he saw Betty leave

Ken's tent and make her way back towards her own area. Once in bed he lay awake for a while wondering about Mrs. Jacks and Mr. Dixon.

★ ★ ★

Next morning at breakfast, Tommy asked innocently, 'What d'you think they were doing?'

The girls giggled and Debbie suggested, 'They might have been kissing or something.'

Tommy shook his head, 'Nah, I think they were just planning what we are all going to do today.'

Tiny looked at him quizzically, 'Ken might be Betty's boyfriend.'

'But she is *Mrs. Jacks* so she must be married, and he also wears a wedding ring.'

All talking at once, the youngsters aired their different views on the situation. The girls decided there was definitely romance in the air.

'Wouldn't it be nice if it's love at first sight, just like in the films,' sighed Margaret.

Her sister smiled, 'I saw the way they were looking at each other, I'm sure there is something going on.'

The boys shook their heads, 'Nah it can't be like that otherwise they wouldn't have wedding rings.'

Further suppositions were interrupted; Betty was shouting from the platform at the front of the marquee, 'Quiet, children, please.' And the children's voices faded into silence. 'The coach will be leaving here at two o'clock tomorrow to take you home, so make the most of today.'

Looking over his glasses, Ken added, 'Don't forget there will be sandwiches for lunch, in here, at one o'clock and dinner is at six o'clock.'

Debbie looked puzzled, 'How can she fancy Ken? He looks so serious and he is a few years older than she is.'

Margaret's eyes shined with excitement, 'It's just like in the films; the men are always older than the girls. I think it's lovely.'

The boys shrugged their shoulders, 'Right, if you've all finished eating let's go.'

Tommy urged, 'We can investigate that field down by the river where the cows are.'

The friends got up to go. 'Come on, I'll race you,' Tommy yelled, and all four ran off through the tents.

Puffing and panting the boys arrived first and collapsed on the ground. The laughing girls caught up with them and falling on top of the boys started to play-fight. 'Let's see if you are ticklish.'

A big, cold nose poked through the fence;

they were face to face with a large black and white cow that lifted her head and mooed loudly. The youngsters jumped up in fright. Tommy slowly reached out and stroked the animal's nose, whilst Debbie looked on in admiration, 'You're brave!'

'It's nothing, I live near the zoo and I'm used to all sorts of wild animals. I even rode a Shetland pony once!'

With a mischievous grin Debbie challenged, 'I bet you can't ride a cow!' Tommy laughed nervously; his need for her admiration overcame any lack of confident, 'Of course I can.'

He climbed the fence and tried to jump on the cow's back. Not being used to such advances, she tossed her head in the air and cantered away to join the rest of the herd. Tommy fell on the grass, quickly recovered, got up and ran after the reluctant beast. Always ready for a game, but unsure about the motives of the scruffy young boy running at them, the cattle started to run in all directions — some towards him. Tommy panicked and, with the girl's screams echoing in his ears, quickly ran towards the river for safety. Jumping in, he waded down towards the fence. As he climbed over, a line of curious cud-chewing cows stood by the river's edge swishing the flies away with their tails, and waiting for the next bit of excitement in an otherwise boring morning.

Debbie hugged him sobbing, 'I didn't mean it, I was only joking!'

The lower half of his body soaking wet, he stood both embarrassed at her show of affection and enjoying the experience.

Tiny looked at him scornfully, 'He was wetter than that when he rode the Shetland pony,' Tommy burst out laughing.

'Can we all join in or is this a private joke?'

Tiny took great pleasure in relating Tommy's previous ignominious attempt at bareback riding as they all sauntered back to the camping area to the accompaniment of his squelching boots.

'I'm going to change. We'll see you girls at lunch, don't forget we're going to meet those gypsies this afternoon.'

★ ★ ★

Jake and his brother were sitting waiting on a tree trunk, waving a bottle at them he beckoned, 'Come and have a drink.'

'What is it?' Tommy asked suspiciously, 'It ain't lemonade, that's for sure!' Seth answered with a grin.

Tommy took a swig; the liquid burned his throat, but he was determined not to show any discomfort. 'Not bad.'

As he handed the bottle back, it gave him great satisfaction to see their looks of disappointment.

Jake passed the bottle to the girls, 'You have a go!'

Debbie grabbed the bottle and took a large mouthful. Grimacing she spluttered, 'It's 'orrible!'

Seth and Jake laughed, 'It's poteen, we make it out of potatoes! It really makes you feel good when you get used to it! Anyone else like some?'

They pushed the bottle towards Margaret and Tiny who both shook their heads, 'Scaredy cats! Right, follow us and we're take you to this quarry. You can really have some good fun there.'

Fifteen minutes or so later, they reached the far side of the woods. And before their eyes was a deep clay and stone quarry with a rusty old railway line leading down into it.

Jake pointed out an even rustier old truck that had been used to bring the aggregates up from the worked seams, 'It's great when you get in that and ride down the rail. It's better'n the fairground!'

Tiny was apprehensive, 'Isn't it dangerous?'

'No! Here have a swig if you're frightened!'

Tiny pulled a face, 'No thanks!'

The truck rattled faster and faster

They walked to the top of the line to investigate the dilapidated contraption. 'There's only room for two. So you boys get in and me and Seth'll hang on the outside. Then we can put our feet down to stop it if it goes too fast. We'll be a sort of protection.'

'Yeah.' Jake added, 'The girls can give it a push and stay at the top and watch.'

The two boys clambered in and with the older boys hanging on either side, Margaret and Debbie chanted, 'Ready, steady, go' and pushed them down the slope.

By the weight of its passengers, the truck accelerated ever downwards. 'Suckers!' Halfway down the gypsy lads jumped off leaving the two boys to their fate. Tommy and Tiny could only cling tightly to its sides, scraping their knuckles on the tunnel walls, as the truck rattled faster and faster towards a dark open mouth. For a few seconds they continued at break-neck velocity into the ever deepening blackness, decelerating indiscernibly as the track levelled out, until CRASH! The truck had ground to a death defying halt. Thrown from their feet, and ricocheting off the sides of the container the two boys banged their heads together and fell in a heap into thick, filthy sludge.

'You OK?'

'Think so,' Tiny sobbed.

'Can't see a thing.'

'Me neither.'

'Let's get out of here.' Tommy wiped away his own tears with the back of his hand and gingerly pulled himself over the side of what could have been their death trap. Cautiously the boys felt their way back up the long tunnel. A pinprick of light guiding them back towards the open air.

When there was sufficient light for a proper inspection of their injuries and he felt a trifle less afraid, Tiny suggested, 'How about a bit of a breather.'

'If you want.'

'What have you done to your face? It's a right bloody mess.'

'Eh! It don't feel too bad. Apart from the bonk we got.' Tommy felt around his face.

'It's your hands.'

'They got pinched between the cart and the wall.'

'Are yer hurt anywhere else?'

'I got a lot of bruises, but look at *your* head. You ain't half got a lump on it and a cut as well.'

His friend felt his head and managed a weak smile, 'So have you! We fell for that one didn't we?'

'We could've been killed!'

'Yeah. We've been very lucky to get away with it.'

Covered in dust and mud, and shielding their eyes against the sun, they made their way to the tunnel entrance and emerged into the daylight.

Tommy's initial shock abated, with anger glinting in his eyes, he looked up and around for the perpetrators of the crime. 'Where's those ruddy gypsies?'

'There they are with the girls! At the top of the slope!'

Even from that distance, it was obvious that whatever they were saying the girls were not happy about it. 'They're trying to drag the girls away.'

'Hey! What d'yer think yer doing?'

'Oi, you! Let go of our girls!' Bruises and cuts forgotten Tommy scrambled up the sleepers. 'Come on, Tiny. We need to teach them two a serious lesson.'

'Wait till I get my hands on that Seth. He's not getting away with treating my girl like that.'

Debbie and Margaret looked round and screamed, 'Help, Tommy!'

'Tiny, Tiny, he's hurting me!'

Seth and Jake looked down to see the two boys approaching fast and took to the woods.

'Thank God you came when you did!' The

terrified girls threw themselves into the arms of their rescuers and clung like frightened children.

'We thought they'd killed you.'

'You are so brave, chasing those big boys like that.'

'Our heroes!'

Tiny was not used to all this praise, 'It was nothing. Anybody would have . . . '

'No, they wouldn't. Those gypsies were massive compared to you.'

'Yeah!' said Tommy pulling a face. 'I reckon arguing with them was more dodgy than taking the truck down the hill!'

'Don't joke, I was scared stiff!'

Tearfully Debbie sniffed, 'They tried to make us go with them to their campsite.'

'And when we refused they got angry and grabbed our hands, trying to force us.'

'We were so worried about you.' Debbie looked at Tommy's head, 'You're bleeding, are you all right?'

He shrugged his shoulders, 'No problem, us London lads are tougher than we look.'

Debbie held him a little bit tighter, 'You don't think they'll come back, do you?'

Tiny shook his head and slowly released Margaret, 'No chance, we'll look after you.'

Tommy smiled, 'Come on let's go back and get cleaned up before dinner.'

And holding Debbie's hand, with Tiny and Margaret whispering and giggling behind them, he led the way back towards their camping site.

★ ★ ★

After dinner the two boys met the girls by the campfire for the final evening's sing-song. Everyone appeared to be a bit depressed, 'Come on, children.' Betty was shouting, 'Let's make the last night a really good one.'

Tommy touched Debbie's hand, 'This time tomorrow we'll all be home.'

She nodded glumly and nudged her sister, 'We'll really miss you two, won't we, Sis?'

Margaret nodded sadly as Tiny put his arm around her waist.

Tommy followed his example by holding Debbie closer and they joined in singing, 'Maybe it's because I'm a Londoner.'

The evening soon passed and it wasn't long before Betty and Ken, side by side, were happily clapping their hands, 'Right everyone! All join in for one last song, and then everyone to bed.'

Debbie nudged Tommy, 'You can see they're in love can't you?'

He shook his head. 'I dunno, I just wonder about their wedding rings. It's a real mystery.'

Then laughed and added, 'Perhaps they gave us false names and they are secretly married, wouldn't that be a surprise!'

They all linked hands and joined in with the singing of 'We'll meet again'.

The evening was getting a bit chilly; Tommy could feel Debbie cuddling up to him to keep warm and noticed her sister was doing the same with Tiny. As the singing finished, Tommy gazed into Debbie's eyes, 'I never thought I would say this to a girl, but I really hope we do meet again, because I'm going to miss you so much.' To his surprise Debbie just pushed her face against his and kissed him fully on the lips. Embarrassed, he looked over her shoulder and he could see Margaret was embracing his friend and kissing him.

Suddenly, Betty and Ken were running towards them, 'Stop it! Stop it!' Then Ken was pulling them apart, 'Go to your tents, now!'

Once inside their tent Tommy very angrily remonstrated with his friend, 'Why are they so angry? I should have told her that I saw her leaving Ken's tent the other night.'

Tiny nodded, 'Yeah, you could really have shown her up in front of everyone.'

Tommy grinned, 'That would have been funny. I would have loved to have seen her face.' Then he reflected, 'Oh well! We had a good time especially being kissed by the girls!'

His friend screwed up his face, 'Yeah, I really enjoyed Margaret kissing me like that, funny 'ennit?'

'I know, I never thought us two would have girlfriends! I mean girls always seemed so soppy, but these two seem so different somehow.'

'I wish they lived near us. Perhaps we can write to them, eh!'

Tommy nodded in agreement, 'Oh well, let's go to bed and we will make the most of tomorrow!'

⋆ ⋆ ⋆

Next day after breakfast the two boys got in the queue for the coach early and saved the back seats. The girls arrived with a huge bunch of bluebells and shepherd's purses. Debbie waved the flowers in recognition and made her way through the noisy youngsters to sit next to Tommy, 'We got up early this morning and collected these for our mum.'

'That's nice. I wish we'd thought of it.'

Once everyone was on board Betty and Ken climbed on and stood at the front of the coach, 'Now children, I hope you tell your parents how much you enjoyed yourselves. We would love to see you all again next year.' She hesitated for a while, 'A few of you misbehaved last night and I'll be having a word with them in a minute, otherwise you have all been very good.'

With all eyes on her, Betty walked down the aisle towards the four youngsters on the back seat. Sitting down between them she pointed her finger at the two boys, 'I don't expect your parents sent you on this holiday to lead these young girls astray, and I've been put in charge to make sure that doesn't happen!'

Margaret interrupted, 'It wasn't their fault, we kissed them! Anyway it was the last night and we were only saying a friendly goodbye.'

Her sister angrily joined in, 'Yeah, it was more us leading them astray, anyway you were in the boys area in Ken's tent the other night and you're both married!'

For a moment or two silence reigned, and a hush fell over the whole coach, before Betty reacted angrily, 'How dare you! We are just friends.'

'Oh, yeah?' Debbie confidently and sarcastically retorted.

Betty burst into tears and Ken rushed down the coach and took her in his arms. 'There! There!'

With tears running down her cheeks she snapped at Debbie, 'I don't have to explain anything to you, but if you must know I'm a widow. Tell them how my husband was killed fighting in the war and you lost your wife when your house was bombed. You children should be ashamed of yourselves for saying such wicked things!'

The four friends looked sheepish and downcast. Their embarrassment increased as Ken explained, 'On the first night of the holiday, I mentioned to Betty that I knew a Private Jacks during the war. He turned out to be her husband. I had some old photographs of me and some army pals in my bag — in my tent. Betty came back with me to look at them.'

Mrs. Jacks interrupted, 'He also told me some lovely stories about my husband that I didn't know. He was able to tell me about my husband's last days. I left his tent feeling happier than I've felt for years. Now you children have spoiled everything.'

'Oh we don't know what to say, we thought . . . '

Tommy's voice tailed off as Ken angrily interrupted. 'That's the trouble you didn't think, did you?'

'We must be fair, dear. It was indiscreet of us. I should have gone and fetched the photographs. If we had met up in the marquee this would not have happened.'

'I suppose so . . . '

'Come on, come and sit with me. We must get moving.' And he led Betty back to the front of the coach under the silent, wide-eyed gaze of all the children.

They sat in embarrassed silence as the coach moved along the winding roads. Tommy shook his head, 'We shouldn't have jumped to conclusions.'

Tiny nodded, 'What can we do about it now?'

Debbie looked crestfallen, 'I feel really, really bad about it. I know, let's all go down and apologise and give her my mum's flowers.' She looked at the others, 'What d'yer think?'

Tommy was uncertain, 'It's not much, but I suppose it's something.'

The other two agreed.

'That's the least we can do!'

The four penitents trooped down the aisle. Debbie said tearfully, 'We're so very sorry, will you accept these flowers with our apologies?'

Betty looked at Ken questionably and he nodded, 'Of course.'

She dried her tears and whispered, 'But let this be a lesson to you. We both miss our loved ones very much, after all this time, and we find talking about them really helps us come to terms with our losses. Both of us are trying to move on in our lives, but we will never let our memories fade. So, like lots of other people, we are just friends brought together by the tragedy of war. As you go through life you'll find things are not always what they seem!'

For the rest of the journey they were in a subdued mood although Debbie kept squeezing Tommy's hand and giving him little gentle kisses on his cheek, and Tiny and Margaret cuddled up close together. 'Can we swop addresses so we can write to each other, Deb?'

Her eyes lit up, 'Of course, I wish we were rich and had a telephone!'

'Fat chance! I don't know anyone with a telephone!'

They swapped addresses and Tommy thought over the last few days. He felt a little bit more grown up, and couldn't believe that Tiny and he had girlfriends. Girls had always seemed a hindrance to their activities, and kissing and all that stuff seemed so soppy. Girls didn't go scrumping or like cricket, in fact they didn't do anything that boys liked doing.

All that had changed over one weekend. It

could be fun having a girlfriend; especially one like Debbie. He enjoyed feeling protective towards her and it felt so good when she held his hand and kissed him. Deep down he felt very despondent as he realised how much he was going to miss her.

Maybe they could meet up in the school holidays, but once he started at his new school it would probably be impossible.

His new school! Regent Street Polytechnic! He had forgotten all about that. And as he sat back with a thoughtful expression on his face he wondered what the future had in store for him. One thing — what his brother Freddie told him all those years ago had come true. Girls can be fun!

THE END

We do hope that you have enjoyed reading this large print book.

Did you know that all of our titles are available for purchase?

We publish a wide range of high quality large print books including:
Romances, Mysteries, Classics
General Fiction
Non Fiction and Westerns

Special interest titles available in large print are:
The Little Oxford Dictionary
Music Book
Song Book
Hymn Book
Service Book

Also available from us courtesy of Oxford University Press:
Young Readers' Dictionary
(large print edition)
Young Readers' Thesaurus
(large print edition)

For further information or a free brochure, please contact us at:
Ulverscroft Large Print Books Ltd.,
The Green, Bradgate Road, Anstey,
Leicester, LE7 7FU, England.
Tel: (00 44) 0116 236 4325
Fax: (00 44) 0116 234 0205

ALLOTTED TIME

Robin Shelton

Robin Shelton was at a crisis point in his life. Divorced, broke and suffering from depression, he and trusty mate Steve decide that they need a project. They decide to take on an allotment . . . What had seemed like a good idea over a couple of beers becomes a daunting task in the cold light of day, when they are faced with a patch of ground so wild Ray Mears might have found it intimidating. But gradually their perseverance pays off and the end of the year finds them wiser, saner — and with an impressive array of crops to boot.

THE RIVER

Philippa Forrester

When TV presenter Philippa Forrester first met Charlie, a wildlife cameraman, she thought he was a show-off — and he thought she was arrogant. The second time, they fell in love. This is the story of the couple's move out of London, and deep into the heart of the English countryside. When they impulsively buy an old mill-worker's cottage, they are entranced by its river, teeming with kingfishers, mink and water fowl. But they are overjoyed when they spot an animal long thought to have abandoned the area: an otter, swimming happily past their house. Inspired, they decide to make a film about the otters, at the same time as having a baby and pursuing their careers . . .

TWO STEPS BACKWARD

Susie Kelly

Susie Kelly and her husband Terry dreamed of a home in France. With their dogs, parrots and horses, they moved to a farmhouse in the Poitou-Charentes region. While Terry worked in England, Susie had to contend with a homicidal gas cooker, burst pipes and a biting guinea fowl. The enormity of what they had taken on seemed overwhelming, and when Terry came close to death, the dream threatened to turn into a nightmare. But the kindness of the local community inspired them to make a new life for themselves in the place they now call home.

BOTSWANA TIME

Will Randall

Botswana, on the edge of the mighty Kalahari desert, is Africa's success story. Since its independence in 1966, the country has built itself into a beacon of wealth and stability. Will Randall found himself in Botswana, resuming a teaching career that had already taken him from an inner-London comprehensive to India. And now that career veers off the beaten track to the tiny town of Kasane. A place that has 'a very good prison' and arguably the best football team in the land. A town where school speech day is attended by a tribe of mongooses, a family of warthogs, a couple of circling eagles and a watchful buffalo — and where Randall learns, mostly through (mis)adventure, all about Botswana.

MOVING MOUNTAINS

Claire Bertschinger

In Ethiopia in 1984, Claire Bertschinger, an International Red Cross nurse, was filmed surrounded by thousands of starving people and with limited supplies. She had the terrible task of choosing which children to feed, knowing that those she turned away might not last the night. Those shocking pictures inspired Bob Geldof: and, ultimately, Live Aid . . . Twenty years later Michael Buerk, whose television reports first showed those pictures, persuaded Claire to return to Ethiopia. Claire had always been haunted by the memory of having to make such terrible choices, but the survivors, calling her 'Mamma Claire', welcomed her back with open arms.